PROJECT
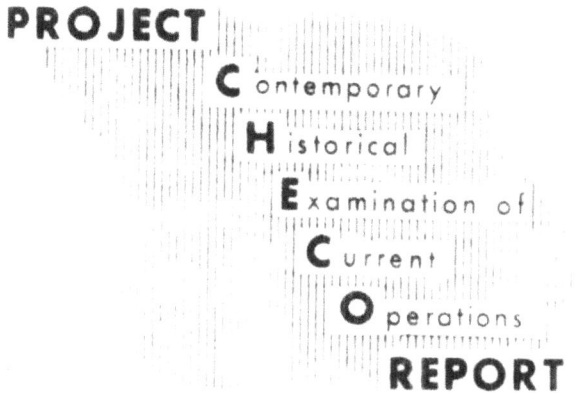

Contemporary
Historical
Examination of
Current
Operations

REPORT

IGLOO WHITE

JANUARY 1970 - SEPTEMBER 1971

1 NOVEMBER 1971

HQ PACAF
Directorate of Operations Analysis
CHECO/CORONA HARVEST DIVISION

Prepared by:
CAPT HENRY S. SHIELDS
Project CHECO 7th AF, DOAC

DEPARTMENT OF THE AIR FORCE
HEADQUARTERS PACIFIC AIR FORCES
APO SAN FRANCISCO 96553

OFFICE OF THE CHIEF OF STAFF

PROJECT CHECO REPORTS

The counterinsurgency and unconventional warfare environment of Southeast Asia has resulted in the employment of USAF airpower to meet a multitude of requirements. The varied applications of airpower have involved the full spectrum of USAF aerospace vehicles, support equipment, and manpower. As a result, there has been an accumulation of operational data and experiences that, as a priority, must be collected, documented, and analyzed as to current and future impact upon USAF policies, concepts, and doctrine.

Fortunately, the value of collecting and documenting our SEA experiences was recognized at an early date. In 1962, Hq USAF directed CINCPACAF to establish an activity that would be primarily responsive to Air Staff requirements and direction, and would provide timely and analytical studies of USAF combat operations in SEA.

Project CHECO, an acronym for Contemporary Historical Examination of Current Operations, was established to meet this Air Staff requirement. Managed by Hq PACAF, with elements at Hq 7AF and 7AF/13AF, Project CHECO provides a scholarly, "on-going" historical examination, documentation, and reporting on USAF policies, concepts, and doctrine in PACOM. This CHECO report is part of the overall documentation and examination which is being accomplished. It is an authentic source for an assessment of the effectiveness of USAF airpower in PACOM when used in proper context. The reader must view the study in relation to the events and circumstances at the time of its preparation--recognizing that it was prepared on a contemporary basis which restricted perspective and that the author's research was limited to records available within his local headquarters area.

ERNEST C. HARDIN, JR., Major General, USAF
Chief of Staff

DEPARTMENT OF THE AIR FORCE
HEADQUARTERS PACIFIC AIR FORCES
APO SAN FRANCISCO 96553

REPLY TO
ATTN OF: DOAD

1 November 1971

SUBJECT: Project CHECO Report, "IGLOO WHITE, January 1970-September 1971"

TO: SEE DISTRIBUTION PAGE

1. Attached is a SECRET document. It shall be transported, stored, safeguarded, and accounted for in accordance with applicable security directives. Each page is marked according to its contents. Retain or destroy in accordance with AFR 205-1. Do not return.

2. This letter does not contain classified information and may be declassified if attachment is removed from it.

FOR THE COMMANDER IN CHIEF

MIKE DELEON, Colonel, USAF
Chief, CHECO/CORONA HARVEST Division
Directorate of Operations Analysis
DCS/Operations

1 Atch
Project CHECO Rprt (S),
1 Nov 71

DISTRIBUTION LIST

1. SECRETARY OF THE AIR FORCE

    a. SAFAA 1
    b. SAFLL 1
    c. SAFOI 2
    d. SAFUS 1

2. HEADQUARTERS USAF

    a. AFNB 1

    b. AFCCS
       (1) AFCCSSA 1
       (2) AFCVC 1
       (3) AFCAV 1
       (4) AFCHO 2

    c. AFCSA
       (1) AF/SAG 1
       (2) AF/SAMI 1

    d. AF/SAJ 1

    e. AFIGO
       (1) OSIIAP 3
       (2) IGS 1

    f. AFSG 1

    g. AFINATC 5

    h. AFACMI 1

    i. AFODC
       (1) AFPRC 1
       (2) AFPRE 1
       (3) AFPRM 1

    j. AFPDC
       (1) AFDPW 1

    k. AFRD
       (1) AFRDP 1
       (2) AFRDQ 1
       (3) AFRDQPC 1
       (4) AFRDR 1
       (5) AFRDQL 1

    l. AFSDC
       (1) AFSLP 1
       (2) AFSME 1
       (3) AFSMS 1
       (4) AFSSS 1
       (5) AFSTP 1

    m. AFTAC 1

    n. AFXO 1
       (1) AFXOB 1
       (2) AFXOD 1
       (3) AFXODC 1
       (4) AFSODD 1
       (5) AFXODL 1
       (6) AFXOOG 1
       (7) AFXOSL 1
       (8) AFXOOSN 1
       (9) AFXOOSO 1
       (10) AFXOOSS 1
       (11) AFXOOSV 1
       (12) AFXOOTR 1
       (13) AFXOOTW 1
       (14) AFXOOTZ 1
       (15) AF/XOX 6
       (16) AFXOXXG 1

3. MAJOR COMMAND

   a. TAC

      (1) HEADQUARTERS
         (a) DO 1
         (b) XP 1
         (c) DOCC 1
         (d) DREA 1
         (e) IN 1

      (2) AIR FORCES
         (a) 12AF
            1. DOO 1
            2. IN 1
         (b) 19AF(IN) 1
         (c) USAFSOF(DO) . . 1

      (3) WINGS
         (a) 1SOW(DOI) . . . 1
         (b) 23TFW(DOI) . . . 1
         (c) 27TRW(DOI) . . . 1
         (d) 33TFW(DOI) . . . 1
         (e) 64TAW(DOI) . . . 1
         (f) 67TRW(DOI) . . . 1
         (g) 75TRW(DOI) . . . 1
         (h) 316TAW(DOX) . . 1
         (i) 363TRW(DOI) . . 1
         (j) 464TFW(DOI) . . 1
         (k) 474TFW(DOI) . . 1
         (l) 35TFW(DOI) . . . 1
         (m) 516TAW(DOX) . . 1
         (n) 4403TFW(DOI) . . 1
         (o) 58TAC FTR TNG WG 1
         (p) 354TFW(DOI) . . 1
         (p) 60MAWG(DOOXI) . 1

      (4) TAC CENTERS, SCHOOLS
         (a) USAFTAWC(DRA). . 1
         (b) USAFTFWC(DRA). . 1
         (c) USAFAGOS(EDA). . 1

   b. SAC

      (1) HEADQUARTERS
         (a) DOX 1
         (b) XPX 1
         (c) DM 1
         (d) IN 1
         (e) NR 1
         (f) HO 1

      (2) AIR FORCES
         (a) 2AF(INCS) 1
         (b) 8AF(DOA) 2
         (c) 15AF(INCE) 1

   c. MAC

      (1) HEADQUARTERS
         (a) DOI 1
         (b) DOO 1
         (c) CSEH 1
         (d) MACOA 1

      (2) MAC SERVICES
         (a) AWS(HO) 1
         (b) ARRS(XP) 1
         (c) ACGS(CGO) 1

   d. ADC

      (1) HEADQUARTERS
         (a) DO 1
         (b) DOT 1
         (c) XPC 1

      (2) AIR DIVISIONS
         (a) 25AD(DOI) 1
         (b) 23AD(DOI) 1
         (c) 20AD(DOI) 1

   e. ATC
      (1) DOSPI 1

f. AFLC

    (1) HEADQUARTERS
        (a) XOX 1

g. AFSC

    (1) HEADQUARTERS
        (a) XRP 1
        (b) XRLW 1
        (c) SAMSO(XRS) 1
        (d) SDA 1
        (e) HO 1
        (f) ASD(RWST) 1
        (g) ESD(XR) 1
        (h) RADC(DOTL) 1
        (i) ADTC(CCN). 1
        (j) ADTC(DLOSL) 1
        (k) ESD(YW). 1
        (l) AFATL(DL) 1

h. USAFSS

    (1) HEADQUARTERS
        (a) AFSCC(SUR) 2

    (2) SUBORDINATE UNITS
        (a) Eur Scty Rgn(OPD-P) 1

i. USAFSO

    (1) HEADQUARTERS
        (a) CSH 1

j. PACAF

    (1) HEADQUARTERS
        (a) DP 1
        (b) IN 1
        (c) XP 2
        (d) CSH 1
        (e) DOAD 6
        (f) DC 1
        (g) DM 1

    (2) AIR FORCES
        (a) 5AF
            1. CSH 1
            2. XP 1
            3. DO 1
        (b) Det 8, ASD(DOASD) . 1
        (c) 7AF
            1. DO 1
            2. IN 1
            3. XP 1
            4. DOCT 1
            5. DOAC 2
        (d) 13AF
            1. CSH 1
        (e) 7/13AF(CHECO) . . . 1

    (3) AIR DIVISIONS
        (a) 313AD(DOI) 1
        (b) 314AD(XOP) 2
        (c) 327AD
            1. IN 1
        (d) 834AD(DO) 2

         (4) WINGS
             (a) 8TFW(DOEA) 1
             (b) 56SOW(WHD) 1
             (c) 366TFW(DO) 1
             (d) 388TFW(DO) 1
             (e) 405TFW(DOEA) 1
             (f) 432TRW(DOI) 1
             (g) 483TAC ALFT WG . . . 1
             (h) 475TFW(DCO) 1
             (i) 1st Test Sq(A) . . . 1

         (5) OTHER UNITS
             (a) Task Force ALPHA(IN) 1
             (b) 504TASG(DO) 1
             (c) Air Force Advisory
                 Gp 1

    k. USAFE
       (1) HEADQUARTERS
           (a) DOA 1
           (b) DOLO 1
           (c) DOO 1
           (d) XDC 1

       (2) AIR FORCES
           (a) 3AF(DO) 2
           (b) 16AF(DO) 1
           (c) 17AF(IN) 1

       (3) WINGS
           (a) 50TFW(DOA) 1
           (b) 20TFW(DOI) 1
           (c) 401TFW(DCOI) 1
           (d) 513TAW(DOI) 1

4. SEPARATE OPERATING AGENCIES

   a. ACIC(DOP) 2
   b. AFRES(XP) 2
   c. AU
      1. ACSC-SA 1
      2. AUL(SE)-69-108 . . . 2
      3. ASI(ASD-1) 1
      4. ASI(HOA) 2
   d. ANALYTIC SERVICES, INC . 1
   e. USAFA
      1. DFH 1
   f. AFAG(THAILAND) 1

5. MILITARY DEPARTMENTS, UNIFIED AND SPECIFIED COMMANDS, AND JOINT STAFFS

    a. COMUSJAPAN 1
    b. CINCPAC (SAG) 1
    c. CINCPAC (J301) 1
    e. COMUSKOREA (ATTN: J-3) 1
    f. COMUSMACTHAI 1
    g. COMUSMACV (TSCO) 1
    h. COMUSTDC (J3) 1
    i. USCINCEUR (ECJB) 1
    j. USCINCSO (J-3) 1
    k. CINCLANT (N31) 1
    l. CHIEF, NAVAL OPERATIONS 1
    m. COMMANDANT, MARINE CORPS (ABQ) 1
    n. CINCONAD (CHSV-M) 1
    o. DEPARTMENT OF THE ARMY (TAGO) 1
    p. JOINT CHIEFS OF STAFF (J3RR&A) 1
    q. JSTPS 1
    r. SECRETARY OF DEFENSE (OASD/SA) 1
    s. CINCSTRIKE (STRJ-3) 1
    t. CINCAL (HIST) 1
    u. MAAG-CHINA/AF Section (MGAF-O) 1
    v. HQ ALLIED FORCES NORTHERN EUROPE 1
    w. USMACV (MACJ031) 1

6. SCHOOLS

    a. Senior USAF Representative, National War College 1
    b. Senior USAF Representative, Armed Forces Staff College 1
    c. Senior USAF Rep, Industrial College of the Armed Forces 1
    d. Senior USAF Representative, Naval Amphibious School 1
    e. Senior USAF Rep, U.S. Marine Corps Education Center 1
    f. Senior USAF Representative, U.S. Naval War College 1
    g. Senior USAF Representative, U.S. Army War College 1
    h. Senior USAF Rep, U.S. Army C&G Staff College 1
    i. Senior USAF Representative, U.S. Army Infantry School 1
    j. Senior USAF Rep, U.S. Army JFK Center for Special Warfare . . . 1
    k. Senior USAF Representative, U.S. Army Field Artillery School . . 1
    l. Senior USAF Representative, U.S. Liaison Office 1

7. SPECIAL

    a. The RAND Corporation 1
    b. U.S. Air Attache, Vientiane 1

ABOUT THE AUTHOR

Captain Shields received his commission in the USAF upon graduation from Franklin and Marshall College, Lancaster, Pennsylvania, in June 1965. He began his active duty in October 1967 after completing a Master's Degree in Russian and East European History at Indiana University. Since that time he has served as a personnel officer and has graduated from the Defense Intelligence School, Anacosta Naval Annex, Washington, D.C. Immediately before becoming a CHECO writer, Captain Shields worked for a year in the Laos Branch of DCS/Intelligence, at Headquarters Seventh Air Force, Tan Son Nhut Airfield, Republic of Vietnam, starting in July 1970.

TABLE OF CONTENTS

		Page
CHAPTER I	- INTRODUCTION	1
	Origins of IGLOO WHITE	1
	Operation of the IGLOO WHITE System	3
CHAPTER II	- IGLOO WHITE IN COMMANDO HUNTS I - VI	9
	Khe Sanh - 1968	9
	COMMANDO HUNT I (Nov 1968-Mar 1969)	9
	SYCAMORE Control	9
	Special Strike Zones	11
	COMMANDO HUNT II (Apr-Oct 1970)	13
	KEYWORD File	14
	COMMANDO HUNT III (Oct 1969-Apr 1970)	15
	COMMANDO BOLT	16
	Panther Team	18
	Flasher Teams	19
	Summary of Panther/Flasher COMMANDO BOLT Results	22
	COLOSSYS	24
	FERRET III	26
	COMMANDO HUNT IV (Apr-Oct 1970)	30
	COMMANDO HUNT V (Oct 1970-Apr 1971)	31
	Traffic Advisory Service	34
	Phase III Sensors	37
	Sensor String "Band" Concept	37
	Night Fixed Targeting Program	38
	X-T Plotter	40
	Lam Son 719	41
	COMMANDO HUNT VI (Apr-Oct 1971)	43
	DART I Transfer	43
	Additional Sensor Channels	43
	COMPASS FLAG	44
	Reactivation of DO	45
	Use of IGLOO WHITE Outside of STEEL TIGER and the RVN	46
	Cambodia	46
	BARREL ROLL	49
	North Vietnam	50

	Page
CHAPTER III - SENSORS, SENSOR-RELATED DEVICES, AND SPECIAL USES	52
EDET III	53
CAEDET	56
RABET II	57
Acoustical Targeting	58
Use of Sensors for Assessing BDA	60
Portatale	61
Portatale in CREDIBLE CHASE	65
Radio Frequency Interference	65
Enemy Attempts to Neutralize IGLOO WHITE Sensors	67
CHAPTER IV - IGLOO WHITE MONITOR AND RELAY AIRCRAFT	70
PAVE EAGLE I	70
PAVE EAGLE II	72
ABCCC as IGLOO WHITE Relay Aircraft	76
C-130B as IGLOO WHITE/COMPASS FLAG Support Aircraft	77
CHAPTER V - DART I AND II AND DUFFLE BAG	79
DART I	79
DART II	85
U.S. Air Force Support of DUFFLE BAG	90
DUEL BLADE	91
BASS	91
Vietnamization of Sensor Programs	92
CHAPTER VI - THE FUTURE OF IGLOO WHITE: COMMANDO HUNT VII AND BEYOND	95
Planning for COMMANDO HUNT VII	95
REGSENSPO	98
MYSTIC MISSION	103
Conclusion	104
APPENDIX I	105
APPENDIX II	111
APPENDIX III	114
FOOTNOTES	116
GLOSSARY	135
RESEARCH NOTE	138

LIST OF FIGURES

FIGURE		Follows Page
1.	Frontispiece	xiv
2.	TFA Installation	3
3.	TFA S-Band Relay Antennae	5
4.	IBM 360/65 Computer	5
5.	GSM and IBM 2250 Console	5
6.	Main Control Room at TFA	6
7.	Audio Technician and Spectrum Analyzer	7
8.	COMMANDO BOLT/SPARKY FAC	17
9.	COMMANDO BOLT Target Display	17
10.	COMMANDO BOLT Operating Areas (COMMANDO HUNT III)	18
11.	GSM Using Light Pen on IBM 2250 Display Console	24
12.	Display of Sensor Activations on X-T Plotter	26
13.	X-T Plotter mounted on EC-121R BATCAT	26
14.	Trucks Destroyed or Damaged (COMMANDO BOLT During COMMANDO HUNT V)	32
15.	HEADSHED Night Traffic Advisory Station	34
16.	Sensor String Deployment Concepts (COMMANDO HUNT V)	37
17.	Sensor String "Bands" during COMMANDO HUNT V	37
18.	Sensor Strings in Cambodia	48
19.	ACOUSID III and ADSID III Sensors	52
20.	EDET III and COMMIKE III Sensors	53

FIGURE	Follows Page
21. Portatale Unit	61
22. January 1970 Portatale Test	63
23. Lockheed EC-121R BATCAT	70
24. Beech QU-22B (PAVE EAGLE II)	72
25. Lockheed C-130E ABCCC	76
26. DART I Operating Locations	79
27. DART I X-T Plotters	83
28. Area Monitored by DART II	85
29. VR Sectors in STEEL TIGER for COMMANDO HUNTs VI and VII	95

LIST OF TABLES

		Page
1.	Effective Detection Ranges of IGLOO WHITE Sensors	6
2.	Panther A-1 Results for COMMANDO HUNT III (COMMANDO HUNT III)	20
3.	Flasher Aircraft Results for COMMANDO HUNT III (COMMANDO HUNT III)	20
4.	A-1 Results Against Trucks in STEEL TIGER (COMMANDO HUNT III)	22
5.	Flasher Aircraft Results Against Trucks in STEEL TIGER (COMMANDO HUNT III)	22
6.	Results of Evaluation of SPOTLIGHT and FERRET III	29
7.	TFA Night Traffic Advisory Service Summary (HEADSHED)	36
8.	DART II Results	89

CHAPTER I

INTRODUCTION

Origins of IGLOO WHITE

IGLOO WHITE originated as part of a September 1966 plan of Secretary of Defense Robert S. McNamara to interdict North Vietnamese infiltration into the Republic of Vietnam (RVN). Originally called PRACTICE NINE, the plan was renamed ILLINOIS CITY, DYE MARKER, and MUSCLE SHOALS before it was finally designated IGLOO WHITE in June 1968. The initial PRACTICE NINE program included two major, closely related subsystems: (1) A Strong Point Obstacle sub-System (SPOS) (later redesignated DUEL BLADE) stretching across the RVN just below the Demilitarized Zone (DMZ) from the coast to the Laotian border; and (2) An air-supported anti-infiltration subsystem stretching westward from the SPOS into Laos to interdict the Ho Chi Minh Trail through central and eastern Laos, by which the enemy supplied his forces in South Vietnam. The Laotian part of the plan envisioned the emplacement of both sensor devises and special munitions to detect and impede this traffic. By July 1968, however, the munitions part of the program had proved to be relatively ineffective, and the use of air-delivered electronic ground sensors for reconnaissance purposes became the primary feature of the system.[1] A special joint task force designated the Defense Communications Planning Group (DCPG) was established by Mr. McNamara to plan and develop this system.[2]

DCPG's original concepts concerning the role and functioning of the new anti-infiltration system differed significantly from those of Seventh Air Force, the operational command responsible for operating MUSCLE SHOALS/IGLOO WHITE and using its data. The DCPG program plan of 25 October 1967 included a strike component consisting of "such elements as Forward Air Controller (FAC) aircraft, strike aircraft, and the Southeast Asia (SEA) Integrated Air Control System."[3/] When discussing MUSCLE SHOALS'/IGLOO WHITE's and the SPOS's objectives, this plan referred to the performance of a "large scale selective interdiction" of the enemy's resupply and support effort and implied that a relatively high priority was attached to the assignment of strike resources to areas covered by MUSCLE SHOALS/IGLOO WHITE.[4/]

The 7AF Operations Plan 481-68 of 10 August 1967, however, viewed MUSCLE SHOALS/IGLOO WHITE as an augmentation of the overall interdiction program, rather than a "substitute for it."[5/] Seventh Air Force regarded the system as functioning basically as an intelligence gathering device, rather than a control center for directing aircraft strikes on specific targets. Actual control of FAC and strike aircraft would be vested in the Seventh Air Force Command Center at Tan Son Nhut Air Base, Republic of Vietnam, and the Airborne Command and Control Center (ABCCC) C-130Es operating over the southern Laos interdiction area (Steel Tiger).[6/] As a result of this arrangement, aircraft frequently were unavailable to investigate and strike MUSCLE SHOALS/IGLOO WHITE detected targets in the early months of the program's operation, because Seventh Air Force or ABCCC were directing resources against other objectives. 7/

Operation of the IGLOO WHITE System

IGLOO WHITE consisted of three main components:

a. Battery-powered sensing devices which detected seismic, acoustical or electrical (radio-frequency energy emitted from vehicle engines) signals generated by the presence of enemy vehicles or personnel. The sensors were either implanted in the ground or were para-dropped and allowed to hang in the upper layers of the jungle canopy.

b. An airborne platform (EC-121R, QU-22B, or C-130) designed to monitor the sensors and either relay the information to a ground facility or have it manually read out by specially trained personnel aboard the aircraft.

c. An Infiltration Surveillance Center (ISC) which received sensor data from the airborne monitor and performed detailed intelligence analysis of enemy movement patterns as well as relayed the information to strike agencies in useable form for immediate action. This facility was provided by Task Force Alpha (TFA) which began operations at Nakhon Phanom Royal Thai Air Force Base (RTAFB), Thailand, on 1 December 1967. 8/

Sensor strings were placed along Lines of Communications (LOCs) which intelligence sources (photographic reconnaissance, FACs, Special Intelligence [SI], etc.) had indicated were actual or potential enemy supply routes. The types of sensors and their exact locations were determined by TFA after consideration of soil composition, the extent of tree canopy, and the possibility that terrain features (or terrain "masking") might interfere with proper monitoring of the sensors by the relay aircraft. 9/

TFA was also responsible for managing the sensor field by assigning a unique radio "signature" or "address" to each sensor to prevent two

Task Force Alpha installation at Nakhon Phanom Royal Thai Air Base

Figure 2.

sensors from broadcasting on the same wave length. At the start of the COMMANDO HUNT VII campaign, there were 40 sensor channels available with 64 separate signatures on each channel. Allowing for a certain number of signatures which had to be kept vacant at all times to enhance signal separation and facilitate sensor management, a maximum field of approximately 200 strings (seven sensors each) was possible.[10/] Three of these channels were permanently assigned to the XXIV Corps sensor field in the RVN (known as DART I), and were managed by that command.[11/]

When sensor-implant coordinates and radio frequencies were determined, the 25th Tactical Fighter Squadron (TFS), Ubon, RTAFB, delivered the sensors on the basis of precomputed Sentinel Lock/Range Navigation (LORAN) coordinates. The F-4s dropped the sensor at a speed of 550 knots from altitudes of between 500 feet and 2,000 feet. A string of up to eight sensors could be implanted on one pass, with the sensors being automatically released at pre-selected intervals. Delivery speeds were faster and release altitudes lower than those used for normal ordnance delivery. The exact location of the sensor was determined afterwards by the use of sensor ballistic tables and photography taken by the F-4 during its delivery run. To effectively detect trucks, sensors generally had to be within 100 meters of the road they were monitoring, although this varied depending on terrain and canopy conditions.[12/]

The most common detection method used by IGLOO WHITE at the time of this report were signals from seismic sensors, although engine-ignition detection devices were being introduced into the system in small numbers. Upon receiving a seismic/ignition indication, the sensor would automatically broadcast a ten second electronic pulse which was received, amplified and then relayed by the monitoring aircraft to TFA through any of five 10 foot, 12 foot or 30 foot diameter S-Band antennae (See Figure 3). From these antennae, the signals were fed into an IBM 360/65 computer (See Figure 4) which in turn displayed the data in usable form on an IBM 2250 display console (See Figure 5). Signals were used by a Ground Surveillance Monitor (GSM), a highly trained officer familiar with the sensor field and the Laotian route structure that was responsible for monitoring a specified group of sensor strings. His task was to combine his experience and judgment with the computerized tools at his disposal to assess sensor activations in order to detect recognizable sequences which would reveal the presence of "movers" (enemy vehicles detected moving along an LOC). The GSM entered confirmed movers into the data base and relayed the information to the TFA control room for possible action.

Seismic/ignition activations were presented electronically to the GSM in a format similar to that used on the Coincidence Filtering Intelligence Reporting Medium (CONFIRM) sheets which were available as print-out copies from the computer (See Appendix I for an explanation of these sheets). The major presentation difference between hard copy CONFIRM sheets and the GSM's 2250 display was that, while the console depicted the past 30 minutes of activations on each string, the sheets showed the last 40 minutes.

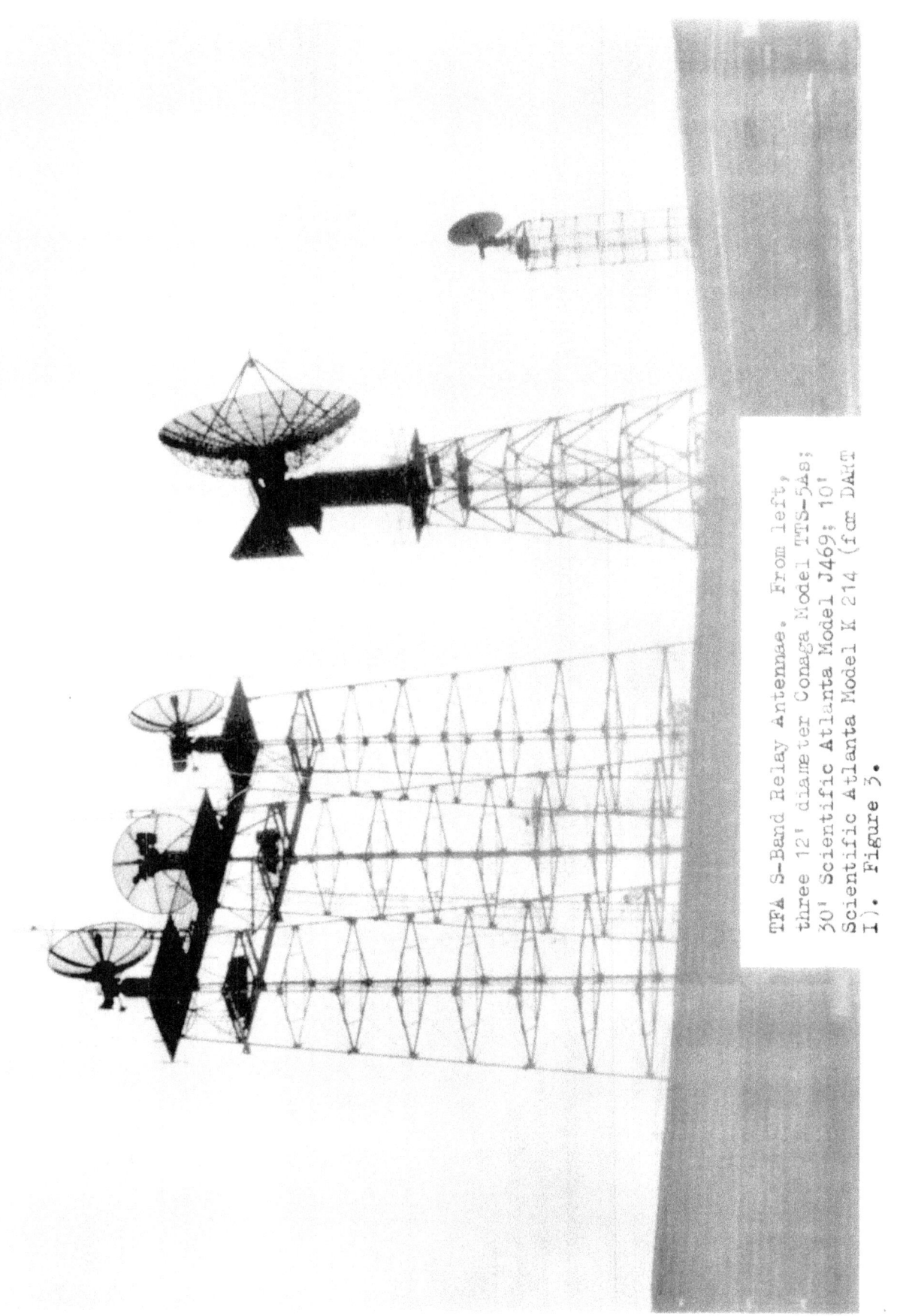

TFA S-Band Relay Antennae. From left, three 12' diameter Conaga Model TTS-5as; 30' Scientific Atlanta Model J469; 10' Scientific Atlanta Model K 214 (from DARM I). Figure 3.

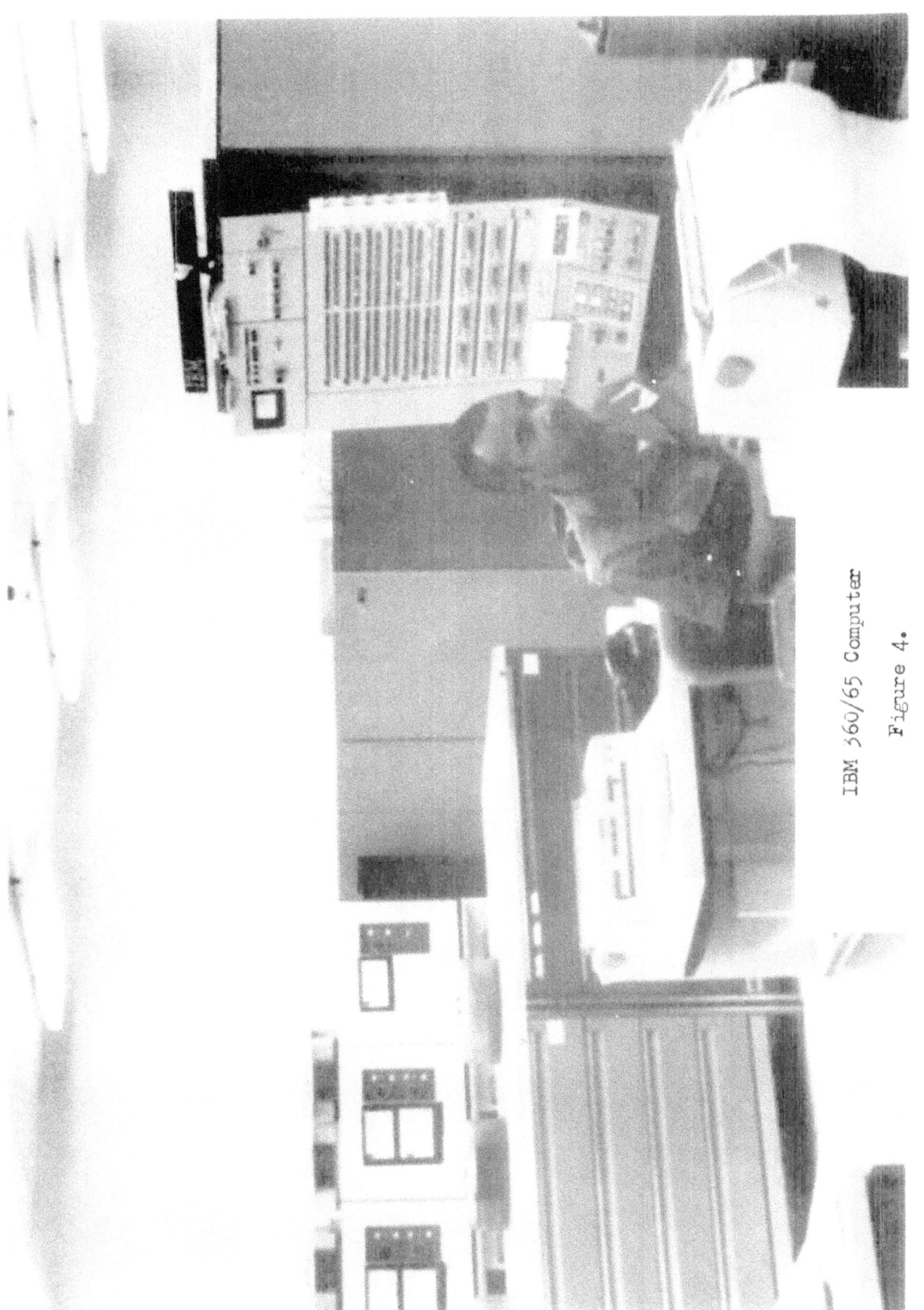

IBM 360/65 Computer

Figure 4.

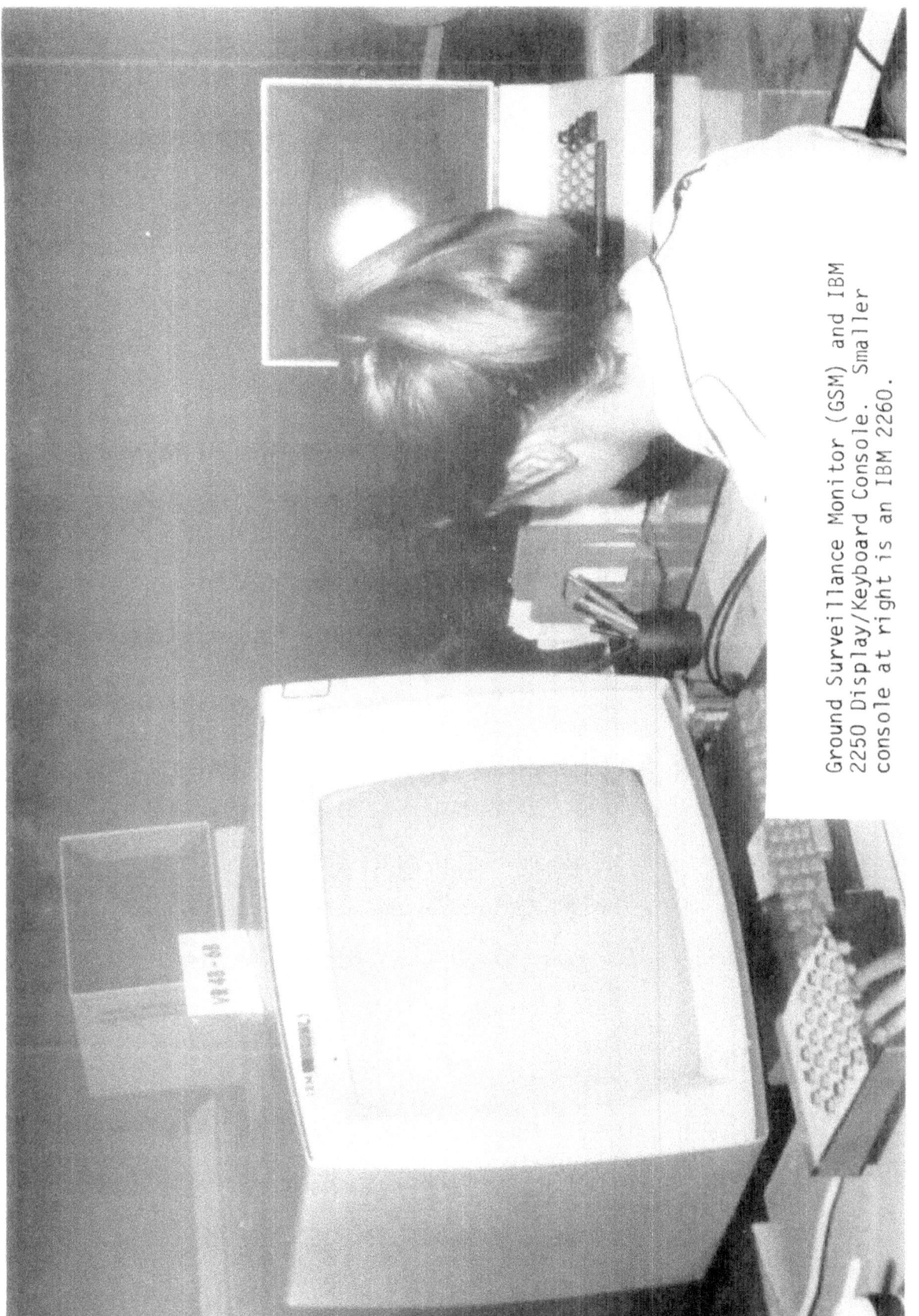

Ground Surveillance Monitor (GSM) and IBM 2250 Display/Keyboard Console. Smaller console at right is an IBM 2260.

FIGURE 5

TABLE 1

EFFECTIVE DETECTION RANGES OF IGLOO WHITE SENSORS [13]

(IN USE FOR COMMANDO HUNT VII)

	Trucks	Personnel
Seismic		
ADSID III	100-150 meters	30-50 meters
Acoustic		
COMMIKE III	300-1500 meters	30-100 meters
Seismic and Acoustic		
ACOUSID III	100-300 meters	30-50 meters
Ignition		
EDET III	100-200 meters	-

The GSM was able to direct the computer to display up to eight sensor strings (depending on the number of sensors in each string) on the 2250 screen as rapidly as he could scan the console display. On nights of heavy activity the sensor field was divided between at least two 2250 consoles/GSMs to facilitate the monitoring of all sensor strings as often as possible.

Acoustic sensors differed from seismic/ignition types in that they sent signals only on command from radio operators in the ISC plot room. Two procedures were followed in "polling" (commanding to send audio)

Main Control Room at TFA
with Wall Display Boards

Figure 6.

acoustic sensors. If a seismic/ignition sensor displayed an activation, the GSM immediately determined if there were active acoustic sensors in the string. If so, he directed the Radio Operator to poll the acoustic sensor in an attempt to determine the nature of the activity. By listening directly to the sounds and using a Spectrum Analyzer to supplement his knowledge and experience, the Radio Operator assessed the source of the sounds and entered this assessment into the computer by means of an IBM 2260 display console/keyboard (See Figure 7). The computer simultaneously entered this assessment onto the 2250 display in front of the GSM. The Spectrum Analyzer (See Figure 7) was basically a cathode ray tube on which were displayed patterns generated by the acoustic signals. Since moving vehicles and aircraft had distinct patterns, the Radio Operator used the highly sensitive analyzer to detect the presence of trucks when their engine sounds were either too faint for the human ear, or were covered by exploding ordnance or aircraft noise.

The second procedure used to monitor acoustic sensors was a random polling by the Radio Operator of selected sensors at 15-30 minute intervals. This was done through the 2260 console at each audio-monitoring station, again by means of the operator's assessment of sounds and use of the Spectrum Analyzer. The number of sensors which could be effectively polled was limited during periods of activity, however, by the operator's tendency to concentrate his attention on COMMIKEs which were showing activations and neglect other acoustic sensors.[14/] By the start of COMMANDO HUNT VII, combinations of acoustic, seismic, and ignition-detection

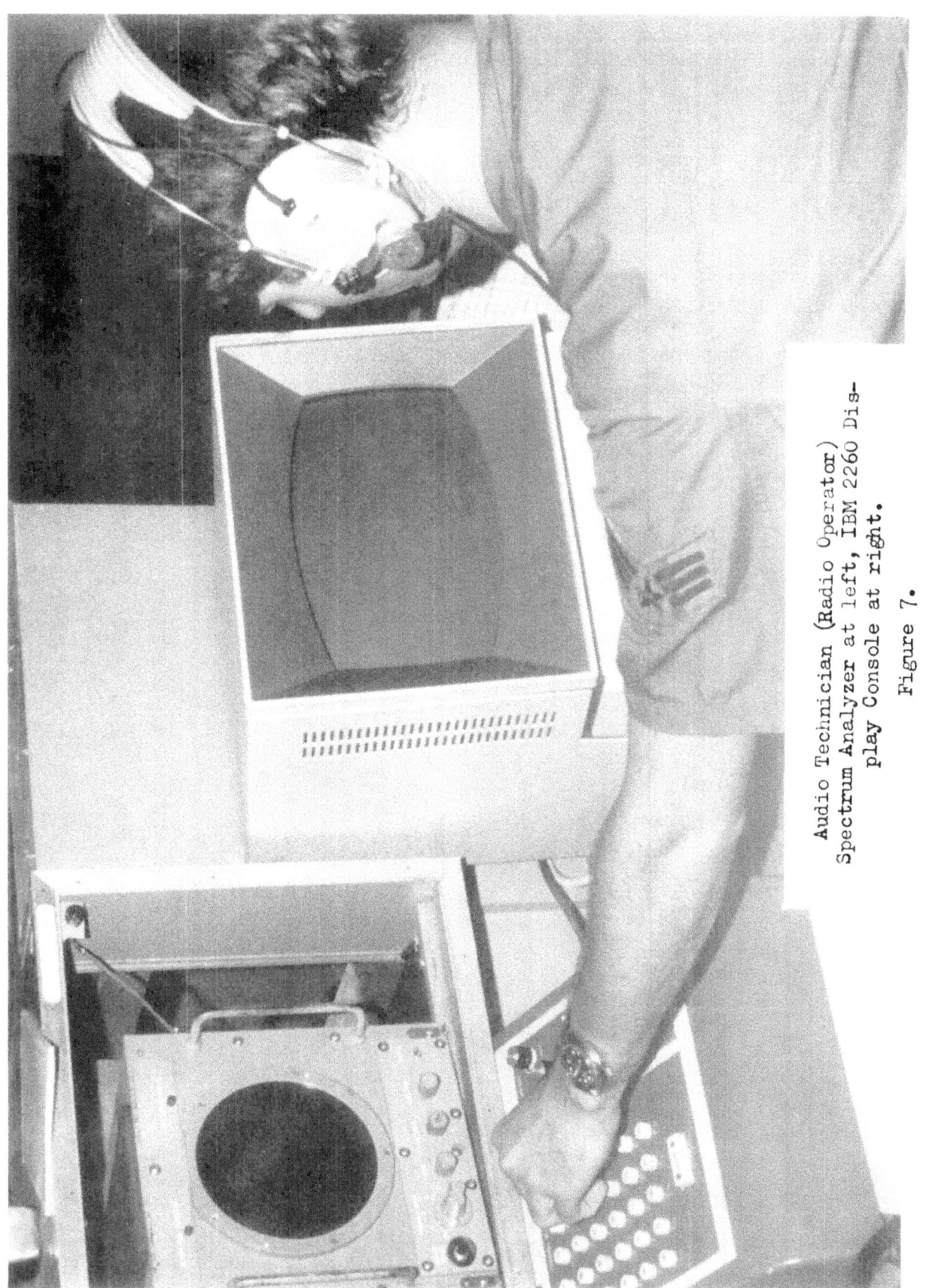

Audio Technician (Radio Operator) Spectrum Analyzer at left, IBM 2260 Display Console at right.

Figure 7.

sensors showed promise of eventually replacing this procedure.

The preceding account of IGLOO WHITE sketches the system's operation as of September 1971. In the following description of IGLOO WHITE's evolution from 1968-1971, these procedures remained generally the same throughout the whole period. Changes which occurred primarily concerned the introduction of new equipment and automated procedures designed to enhance the effectiveness of existing procedures and automate previously manual operations.

CHAPTER II

IGLOO WHITE IN COMMANDO HUNTS I-IV

Khe Sanh - 1968

The IGLOO WHITE concept of detecting enemy movement by remotely monitored ground sensors was first used operationally in January 1968 during the seige of Khe Sanh. TFA monitored sensors were used throughout this campaign in northern RVN to direct air and artillery strikes and obtain intelligence about enemy movements. As a result of experience gained at that time, TFA found it necessary to refine its capability to differentiate between sensor activations caused by friendly ordnance and those resulting from enemy activity. [15/]

COMMANDO HUNT I (Nov 1968 - Mar 1969)

SYCAMORE Control. During this campaign 7th Air Force revised its previous position and assigned TFA operational control of designated strike aircraft in the COMMANDO HUNT area (STEEL TIGER north of 16°30') [16/] as a function complementary to its target development and truck counting activities. TFA was expected to provide these aircraft with targets by "rapidly" exploiting IGLOO WHITE information. A Combat Operations Center (COC) known as SYCAMORE Control was activated at TFA in October 1968 to accomplish this, and was designed to function "...as an extension of the 7th Air Force Command Center for the direct control of all air resources within the Commando Hunt area." [17/] To expedite the operational effectiveness of the TFA COC, controllers from the Airborne Command and

Control Center (ABCCC) aircraft based at Udorn RTAFB were assigned TDY to TFA to assist SYCAMORE Control personnel. ABCCC controllers retained operational direction of strike aircraft in northern Laos (BARREL ROLL) and in southern STEEL TIGER outside of the COMMANDO HUNT area. [18]

Lucrative moving targets were called by phone to the intelligence team in the SYCAMORE Control center by the Traffic Assessment Officers (TAO, later Ground Sensor Monitors). These officers identified enemy truck sequences and patterns from computer-produced CONFIRM sheets, since IBM 2250 and 2260 display consoles had not yet been introduced at TFA. [19]

These sheets covered all active sensors and were updated every five minutes. [20] Depending upon the value of the target, FAC availability, the current tactical situation, and weather in the target area, potential targets were passed to the FAC controller and then to an on-station FAC as a target nomination. [21] These nominations were called SPOTLIGHT reports. [22] In cases where the sequence fell outside of the direct SYCAMORE Control/COMMANDO HUNT area, the information was passed via secure voice circuit to the appropriate ABCCC, where the on-board intelligence officer again determined whether to pass the target to strike aircraft depending on the tactical situation. [23]

Localized-activity sequences frequently indicated the presence of fixed targets (truck parks, transshipment points, etc.). These were given to the Target Intelligence Officer (TIO) who had access to past

IGLOO WHITE, FAC, road-watch team, and photographic interpretation reports, by which he determined the value of the target. If the lead appeared promising, it was repassed to SYCAMORE Control as a recommended target.[24]

Difficulties with SYCAMORE Control's SPOTLIGHT procedures arose as the campaign progressed. The long time lag from the initial sensor activation, to interpretation by the TAO, to relay to the controller, and from him to FAC and strike aircraft frequently resulted in the target having disappeared by the time ordnance arrived in the area.[25] An attempt to correct this shortcoming led to the Special Strike Zone (SSZ) concept, which in many respects was a direct predecessor of the future COMMANDO BOLT and Traffic Advisory Service programs.

Special Strike Zones (SSZ). The SSZ concept had been considered in early IGLOO WHITE planning, but the imperative need for anti-infiltration systems in the RVN and Laos precluded operational testing. As finally implemented in December 1968, groups of three sensor strings (of three to six sensors each)[26] were implanted along selected LOCs so as to detect not only the presence of traffic, but convoy location, size, direction, and speed as well. Careful analysis of the CONFIRM sheets enabled a prediction of the future location of the convoys. This information was passed through the COC to the airborne FAC who would locate the convoys and direct strike aircraft against them.[27]

Starting in March and April 1969 bombing based on Long Range Navigation (LORAN) coordinates was teamed up with the SSZ concept to further refine the use of real time IGLOO WHITE information:[28]

> *By time-tracking trucks along sensor strings, a strike could be made at predicted intercept points by aircraft equipped with accurate navigation equipment and area munitions... As enemy convoys proceeded through the SSZ sensor strings, an estimated time of arrival at the intercept point was relayed form the ISC to the ABCCC controlling strikes for that area. F-4 aircraft....were brought...to the intercept zones by the use of... LORAN equipment in the lead aircraft. When directly over the intercept point, at the time when the trucks were predicted to arrive, CBU-24 munitions were ripple released, spreading BLU bomblets over a wide area to destroy trucks and supplies.*

In anticipation of deteriorating weather in the approaching Southwest Monsoon Season (COMMANDO HUNT II), this system was further developed to improve the ability to allow strikes without visual target acquisition by the pilot.[29]

Towards the end of COMMANDO HUNT I, the decision was made to discontinue SYCAMORE Control, and terminate TFA's role as a direct controller of strike aircraft. SYCAMORE Control had experienced difficulty in communicating with aircraft operating in the southeast portion of its area, and had been forced to relay information through other aircraft. The communications range of the ABCCC aircraft corrected this problem, so control of the entire interdiction area was turned over to airborne controllers.[30]

The COMMANDO HUNT report of 20 May 1969 summed up the role of IGLOO WHITE in the 1968-69 campaign:[31]

> *IGLOO WHITE sensor information assisted in the nightly deployment of the force to the most lucrative route segment. Sensor information was also used effectively to assist FACs in locating larger convoys. In real-time, IGLOO WHITE information was available to FACs, strike aircraft and gunships when they were not otherwise occupied with targets. When this occurred and IGLOO WHITE information was used, it was demonstrated to be an accurate means of locating enemy traffic. It directly assisted in the real-time location of slightly more than 20 percent of the targets attacked.*

COMMANDO HUNT II (Apr - Oct 1970)

Operational control was not officially turned over to the ABCCCs until 13 April 1969, after the formal conclusion of the COMMANDO HUNT I campaign. SYCAMORE Control continued to function as a backup in case the ABCCC proved unable to handle the increased traffic, but ABCCC encountered no difficulties of this kind. TFA's command and control function finally terminated on 26 April,[32] although plans apparently existed at that time to reactivate this capability at the start of COMMANDO HUNT III.[33] The rest of IGLOO WHITE's Southwest Monsoon (wet) season effort was devoted to maintaining certain key sensor fields to detect any enemy supply efforts, and developing the SSZ concept to allow LORAN-equipped F-4s to execute nonvisual strikes on moving convoys, based on sensor-derived real-time information.[34]

KEYWORD File. Of major importance for the future of TFA and IGLOO WHITE was the introduction during COMMANDO HUNT II (in May 1969) of a computerized listing of target information designated the KEYWORD File. This file contained information vital to coordinated target development in a centralized and usable form on short notice, and facilitated the fusion of sensor data with other intelligence sources. As of September 1971, seven functional categories of information made up the file: [35/]

    a. General intelligence category: Initial and supplementary photographic interpretation reports, FAC mission summaries, FAC bulletins and Controlled American Source (CAS) reports.

    b. Tac Air function: Nomination, strike, and bomb damage assessment (BDA) data for tac air targets.

    c. Arc Light category: Nomination, strike, and BDA data for B-52 targets.

    d. Night-targeting category: Nomination, strike, and BDA data for the night-fixed targeting program.

    e. Fac Liaison Program (FACLO) category: TFA visual reconnaissance (VR) requests and resulting responses from FACs concerning eastern STEEL TIGER as well as other information generated by FACs on areas of interest. Also includes route status information based on FAC VR.

    f. Sensor data: Information which indicated the presence of localized, fixed, or semifixed target activity such as truck parks, storage areas, transshipment points, and road repair work. Sensor data which did not provide such leads was not included.

    g. Special Intelligence (SI) category: Information of this kind was not entered into the file, but the presence of SI backup for a particular target area was indicated.

The KEYWORD File was used for target development during the three hours each day that the computer was available for this program. If photographic, FAC, SI, or sensor reports indicated a possible target area during periods when the computer was engaged in other tasks, a daily print out containing the last 30 days of inputs into the File was always available for determining the extent of observed activity within a specified distance of the point. Based upon this history of the area, a decision was made whether to initiate strike nominations, recommend further VR of the areas, or take no action at that time.

The KEYWORD File also served as an accounting and evaluation device and recorded the number of areas nominated by the various targeting programs, the number of strikes, and the resultant BDA. In addition, the KEYWORD File was used to justify requests for photography if the File showed a high level of activity in an area not recently covered.[36/] The anticipated expansion of the KEYWORD File for the COMMANDO HUNT VII campaign is discussed in Chapter VI.

COMMANDO HUNT III (Oct 1969 - Apr 1970)

In COMMANDO HUNT III, IGLOO WHITE built on lessons learned in the previous campaigns and became an integral part of the interdiction effort in STEEL TIGER.[37/] Aircraft command and control responsibilities were not returned to TFA for this campaign, and emphasis instead was placed upon intelligence gathering and targeting.[38/] The most significant event during COMMANDO HUNT III was the introduction of a refined and improved SSZ concept designated COMMANDO BOLT. This program analyzed real time sensor data to obtain future locations of enemy convoys to which strike aircraft could be directed. Like the SSZ program, targets were passed for both visual and LORAN strikes. A certain number of FAC and strike aircraft were fragged directly to TFA each night to operate against COMMANDO BOLT targets.

COMMANDO BOLT. The basis of the COMMANDO BOLT operation was a minute-by-minute monitoring of sensor activations within specially designed sensor strike strings. As soon as vehicle movement was detected within one of the strings, the activity was monitored by a SPARKY FAC team located on the balcony of the TFA control room. SPARKY FAC consisted of the following three-man team: 39/

    a. Strike Nominator: An intelligence officer experienced in assessing sensor-derived data who monitored real time sensor activations on an IBM 2250 console and determined the number, direction, and velocity of potential targets by means of continuously up-dated displays. The 2250 console and data display were identical to those used by CSMs to monitor the entire sensor field. The SPARKY FAC display, however, monitored only COMMANDO BOLT strings.

    b. Strike Controller: An experienced field grade fighter pilot familiar with tactical aircraft capabilities and trained in the interpretation of sensor-derived data. His duties were to direct night FACs and strike aircraft to sensor-revealed truck movements on a real time basis in order to deliver attacks. He was also responsible for coordinating aircraft employment with ABCCC and 7th Air Force Command Post.

    c. Strike Technician: An enlisted technician trained in ground-air radio procedures responsible for monitoring radio transmissions, relaying instructions and information to ABCCC, maintaining data logs, and assisting the strike controller.

Central to the COMMANDO BOLT system were specially designed sensor strings normally consisting of from three to six sensors.[40] These sensors were emplaced at intervals of approximately 200 meters along an LOC segment which had been observed receiving heavy enemy truck traffic. Sometimes as many as four strings were placed along a certain route to form a COMMANDO BOLT "strike module." Desired Mean Points of Impact (DMPI) were located by LORAN coordinates at certain intervals along the strike module. When the sensors revealed the presence of enemy vehicles moving through the module, the large number of sensors allowed the direction and speed of the vehicles to be calculated by the computer so as to obtain an estimated time of arrival (ETA) at a pre-selected DMPI through which they would pass. The newly-installed Coordinated LORAN Sensor Strike System (COLOSSYS) enabled the computer to perform these tasks, and made available to the SPARKY FAC team graphic displays of the route system showing locations of sensors, strike modules, DMPIs and moving targets. These displays could be presented on the 2250 console (See Figures 8 and 9).[41]

Upon obtaining a target ETA the Strike Controller alerted FAC or strike aircraft, specifically assigned to COMMANDO BOLT, to the developing target and passed a Time on Target (TOT) for the DMPI coinciding with the previously determined ETA. The pilot entered the LORAN coordinates for the specified DMPI into his on-board computer and then adjusted the speed or flight path of his aircraft so that his TOT would

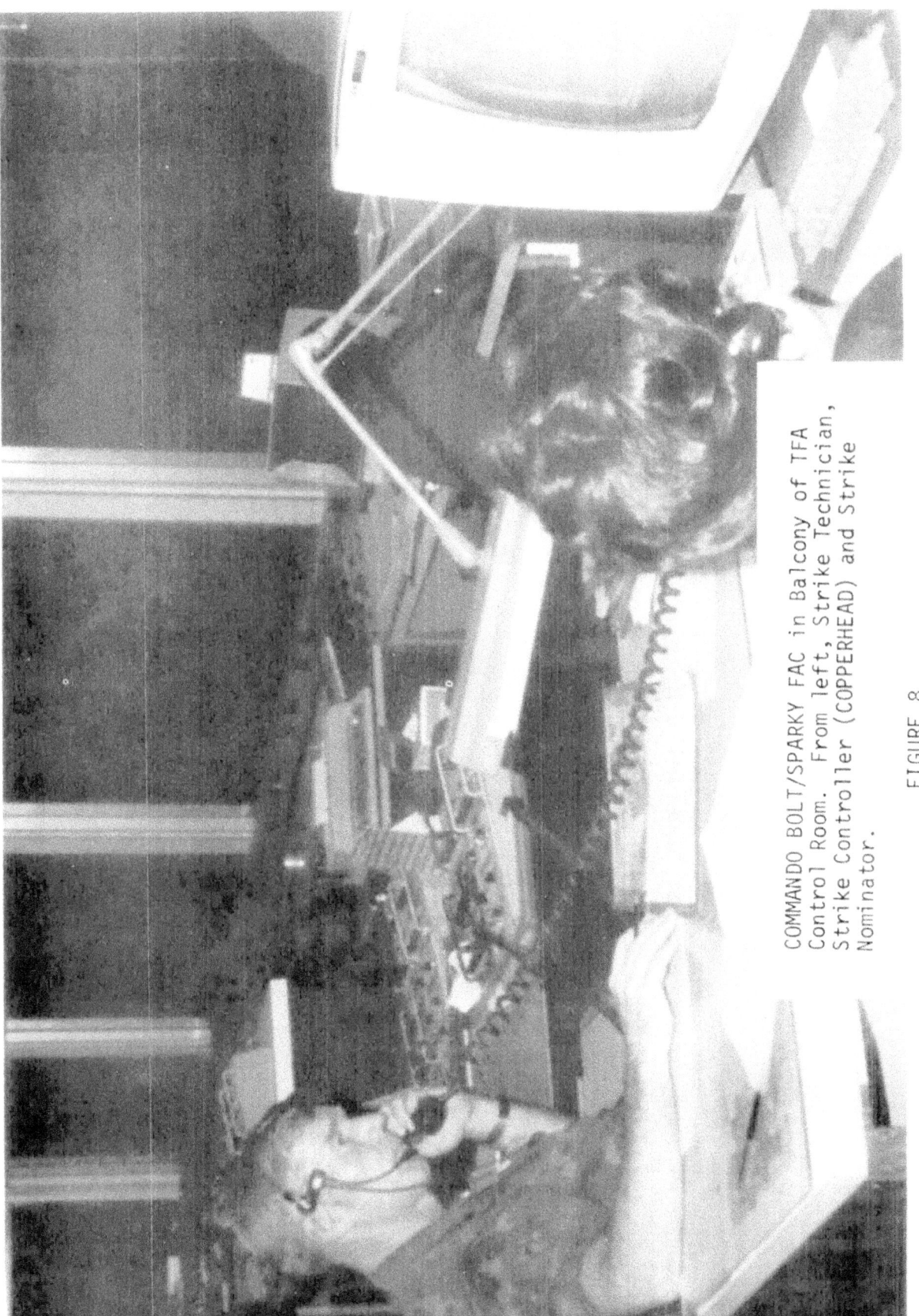

COMMANDO BOLT/SPARKY FAC in Balcony of TFA Control Room. From left, Strike Technician, Strike Controller (COPPERHEAD) and Strike Nominator.

FIGURE 8

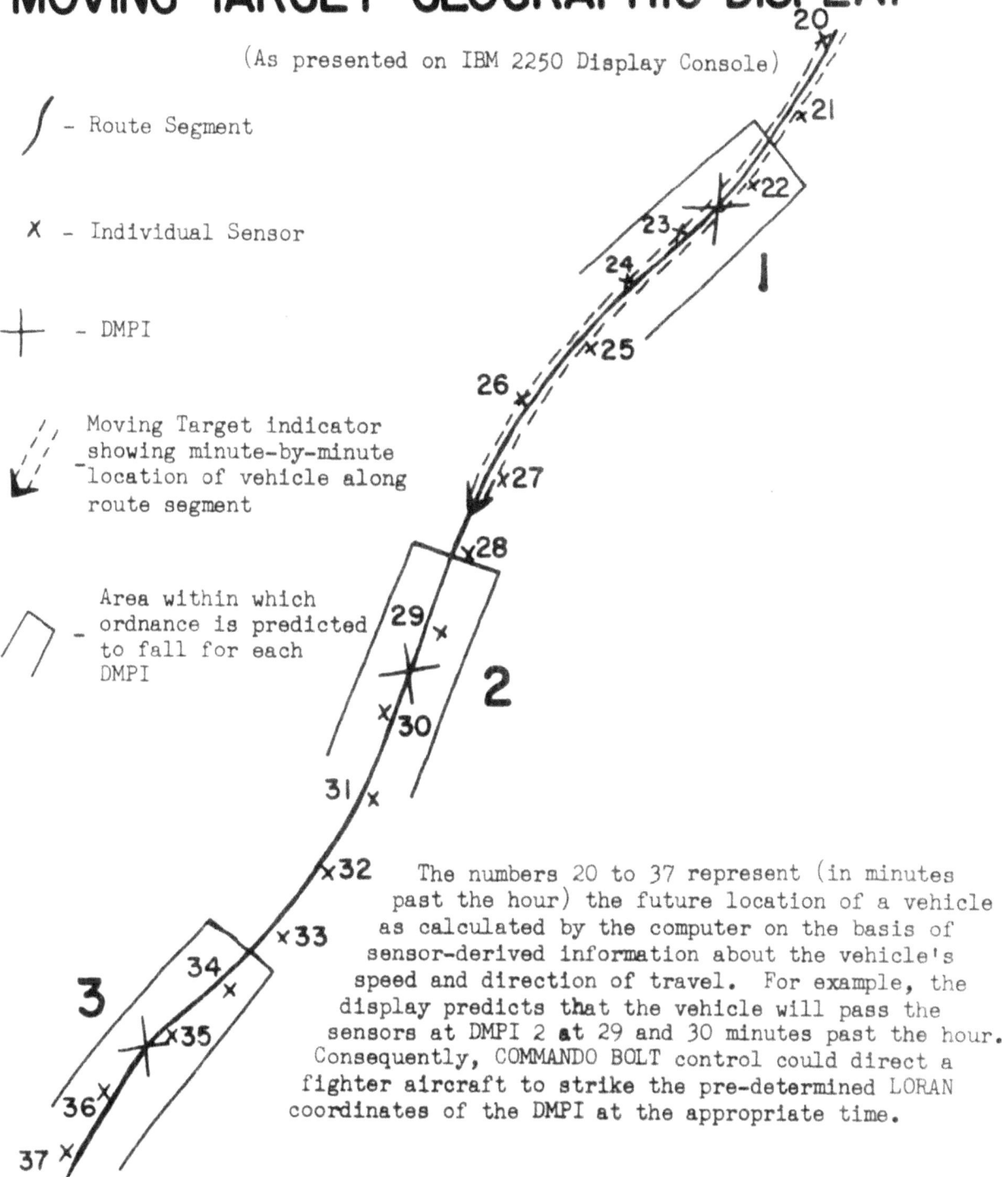

FIGURE 9

coincide with TFA's TOT. The Strike Nominator continually monitored the progress of the target through the module and revised the ETA/TOT if changes in speed were observed. Flights of aircraft designated Panther and Flasher Teams were assigned to operate on the basis of SPARKY FAC sensor-derived target intelligence.[42]

Panther Team. A Panther Team consisted of any strike aircraft operating with a FAC to attack sensor-detected targets, although it originally consisted of an OV-10 or O-2 night FAC equipped with a Night Observation Device (NOD) and accompanied by two A-1 strike aircraft. When a vehicle target was detected by SPARKY FAC, an ETA/TOT for the appropriate Panther Point (a DMPI associated with all sensor strings) was transmitted to FAC and strike aircraft assigned to COMMANDO BOLT by ABCCC. If the FAC was able to acquire the trucks visually, he marked the target for strike aircraft and standard night strike tactics were followed. If additional ordnance was required the FAC requested it through the TFA COMMANDO BOLT control center (call sign COPPERHEAD) which coordinated the request with ABCCC.[43]

Panther Teams initiated COMMANDO BOLT operations on 20 November 1969 in an area near Ban Karai Pass designated CB-1 (See Figure 10). Three FAC and eight A-1 aircraft normally provided continuous strike coverage from 1815 to approximately 2315 hours Laos time. Increasing North Vietnamese Antiaircraft Artillery (AAA) defenses and adverse weather forced the Panther Teams to abandon CB-1 on 21 December and move their operations to a CB-2 area north of the previous one. The teams operated in CB-2 from 26 December 1969 to 6 February 1970 when

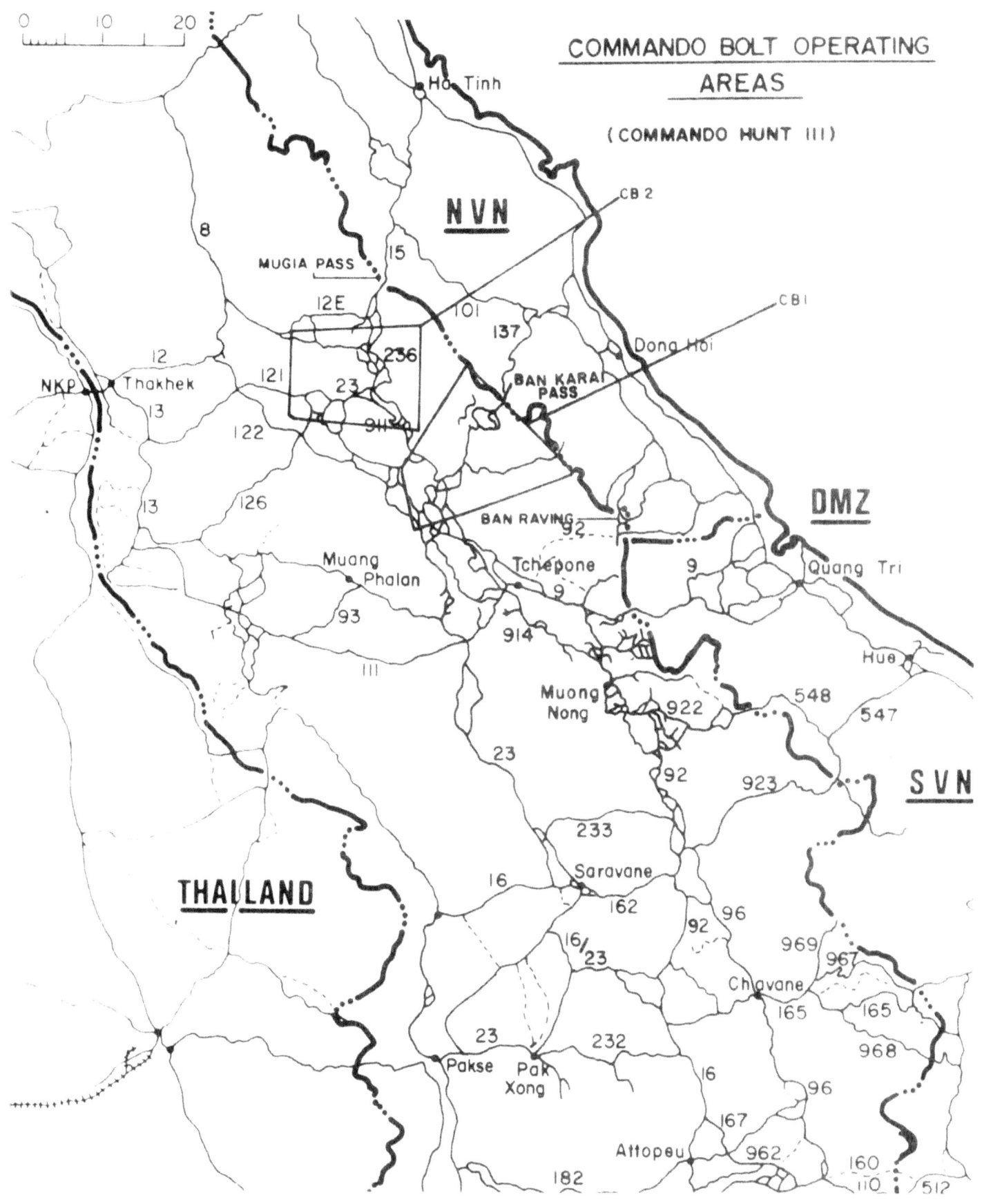

FIGURE 10

air space overcrowding resulting from the employment of gunships in the area forced Panther Teams to terminate operations there also. On 7 February, Panther Teams returned to CB-1 for the remainder of the campaign, although recurring hazards of adverse weather and enemy AAA activity restricted operations to its southern part.[44/]

From 20 November 1969 to 30 April 1970 A-1s flew 378 COMMANDO BOLT sorties, although the number of days that these aircraft were employed in COMMANDO BOLT operations was reduced by bad weather, Search and Rescue (SAR) diversion, and the requirement to support operations in BARREL ROLL.[45/] Table 2 summarizes the results of the 378 COMMANDO BOLT A-1 strikes.

Flasher Teams. Flasher Teams consisted of LORAN or Airborne Moving Target Indicator (AMTI)-equipped F-4s or A-6s operating directly with SPARKY FAC under nonvisual conditions against sensor-detected targets. On occasion aircraft without LORAN and AMTI apparatus accompanied those so equipped and dropped their ordnance on signal from the lead aircraft. These teams became operational on 24 November 1969, with Air Force LORAN F-4s leading other aircraft in strikes in the CB-1 area. Navy and Marine A-6s began operations on 4 and 6 December, respectively, and the program was expanded to CB-2 on 26 December.[46/]

TABLE 2

COMMANDO BOLT

PANTHER A-1 RESULTS FOR COMMANDO HUNT III [47]

Type Target	Destroyed and Damaged	Secondaries
Trucks	164	466
Truck Parks & Storage Areas	-	22
AAA	1	20

TABLE 3

COMMADO BOLT

FLASHER AIRCRAFT RESULTS FOR COMMANDO HUNT III [48]

Type Target	Destroyed and Damaged	Secondaries
Trucks	888	2055
Truck Parks & Storage Areas	-	478
AAA	26	131

Due to the stereotyped nature of COMMANDO BOLT Flasher operations directed against the same DMPIs day after day, enemy AAA defenses in the target area underwent a steady buildup. Flak-suppression sorties by Navy A-7s and Marine F-4s accompanied A-6 Flasher missions, while

Marine EA-6s provided Electronic Countermeasures (ECM) support. These measures gave only temporary relief, however, as the predictability of COMMANDO BOLT target areas encouraged intense and accurate AAA opposition.[49/]

During the course of the campaign, substantial evidence accumulated that the enemy was monitoring strike frequencies and reacting to intercepted transmissions. Although DMPIs were designated by a code name which was changed daily, this was compromised as soon as a DMPI was struck. In early February 1970 secure voice cipher was instituted for transmitting target and strike information, and special mission encoders were used to encode DMPIs and TOTs for aircraft without cipher equipment. Simultaneous with this action enemy AAA accuracy decreased and after 20 February, the Navy discontinued flak suppression sorties.[50/]

Flasher aircraft began working with Panther FACs during February 1970. From 24 November 1969 to 30 April 1970, Flasher aircraft flew a total of 3920 sorties, 361 of which were in support of Panther operations.[51/] Flasher results for COMMANDO HUNT III are presented in Table 3.

Since Flasher Team strikes were often conducted against non-visual targets (obscured by darkness or weather) with ordnance released on specific LORAN coordinates, damage assessment was often hampered and sometimes impossible.[52/]

Summary of Panther/Flasher COMMANDO BOLT Results. Table 4 compares the results of Panther A-1 strikes against trucks with similar BDA obtained by other A-1s. The Panther A-1 teams achieved a slightly lower overall kill rate than did other A-1s operating against enemy trucks, although Panther truck kills were 78 percent higher than other A-1s during January 1970 operations in CB-2. Flasher aircraft overall truck kill rate was 88 percent of that of all other F-4s, A-6s and A-7s, in spite of being 27 percent higher during February.[53/] These results are summarized in Table 5.

TABLE 4

A-1 RESULTS AGAINST TRUCKS IN STEEL TIGER[54/]

COMMANDO HUNT III

	Nov	Dec	Jan	Feb	Mar	Apr	Total
Sorties							
Panther A-1s	34	54	82	70	54	52	346
Other A-1s	249	431	575	320	148	263	1986
Trucks Destroyed/Damaged							
Panther A-1s	5	14	86	45	14	20	184
Other A-1s	112	201	340	189	83	162	1087
Destroyed/Damaged per Sortie							
Panther A-1s	.15	.26	1.05	.64	.26	.38	.53
Other A-1s	.45	.47	.59	.59	.56	.62	.55

TABLE 5

FLASHER AIRCRAFT RESULTS AGAINST TRUCKS IN STEEL TIGER[55]

COMMANDO HUNT III

	Nov*	Dec	Jan	Feb	Mar	Apr	Total
Sorties							
Flasher Aircraft	83	639	1032	481	462	381	3078
Other F-4, A-6, A-7	541	1291	1464	1625	1357	1202	7480
Trucks Destroyed/Damaged							
Flasher Aircraft	8	173	287	204	97	119	888
Other F-4, A-6, A-7	158	390	486	539	474	407	2454
Destroyed/Damaged per Sortie							
Flasher Aircraft	.10	.27	.28	.42	.21	.31	.29
Other F-4, A-6, A-7	.29	.30	.33	.33	.35	.34	.33

*F-4 only

TFA's command and control role in COMMANDO BOLT differed from that in SYCAMORE Control primarily by restricting SPARKY FAC's authority only to aircraft operating in support of the strike modules. During COMMANDO HUNT I, TFA exercised direct control over all aircraft operating in the interdiction area. Under COMMANDO BOLT, however, ABCCC retained control of the gunships and all FAC and strike aircraft not specifically fragged to SPARKY FAC. TFA continued to provide ABCCC with SPOTLIGHT reports of vehicles passing through other sensor strings in STEEL TIGER; however, TFA could only advise that the activity was occurring, and had no authority to order aircraft to that location.

Coordinated LORAN Sensor Strike System (COLOSSYS). The introduction of COLOSSYS into IGLOO WHITE during COMMANDO HUNT III automated previously manual operations and formed the basis of the COMMANDO BOLT and HEADSHED systems. A principal feature of COLOSSYS was an IBM 2250 display console which was capable of projecting constantly updated CONFIRM sheet-type displays of all active sensor strings as rapidly as the Ground Sensor Monitor (GSM) could scan the console screen. These displays were updated every minute and reflected the past 30 minutes of activity on each string. This allowed a GSM to observe continually all sensor inputs (seismic, acoustic, and ignition) from the portion of the sensor field selected for his station. Formerly, seismic and acoustic activations were read from printed CONFIRM sheets which were updated every five minutes for each sensor string.

COLOSSYS displays allowed sensor activations to be monitored on a minute-by-minute basis by use of the same diagonal "step" patterns used on CONFIRM sheets. Since the COLOSSYS display indicated the type and reliability of sensors in each string, the GSM was able to determine whether acoustic sensors were present, and, if so, to request an audio assessment from the radio operator to verify further the nature of the activation. If the sequence passed these tests and was accepted as a mover, a touch of a light pen to the console screen (See Figure 11) would command the computer to calculate the number of movers, their speed, and their direction. Based on the number and duration of the

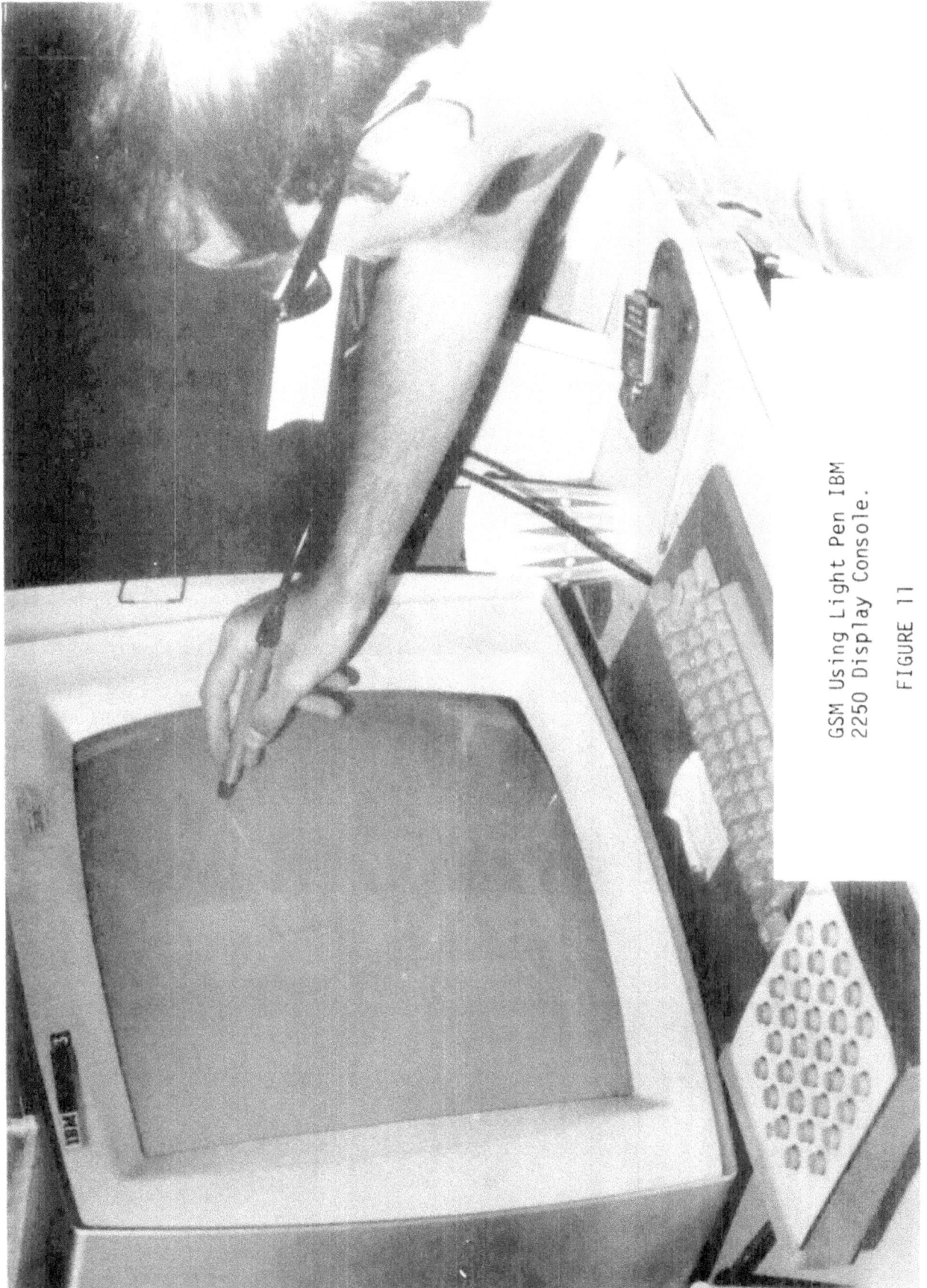

GSM Using Light Pen IBM
2250 Display Console.

FIGURE 11

sensor activations, the GSM would also determine the number of movers in the sequence, and compare his estimate with that of the computer. In case of conflict, the GSM would override the computer and adjust its assessment to agree with his own, insuring that the analytical judgment and background of the operator were always the final authority. The total number of movers detected by the GSMs was incorporated into the ISC Traffic Summary for that night. At the same time as the sequence was entered into the data base, the same touch of the light pen instantaneously transferred all information on the mover(s) to the TFA control room for possible HEADSHED Traffic Advisory Action.

COLOSSYS also made possible the graphic displays of route segments, sensor locations, moving targets, and DMPIs which were used to determine the TOT for COMMANDO BOLT strikes. While a real time strike operation could be run from manual print outs or X-T Plotters, the number of COMMANDO BOLT and HEADSHED advisories which could be issued would be drastically reduced, and many of these would not reach strike aircraft until the target had left the vicinity of the string. Real time targeting could possibly be conducted in a manual mode on nights with small numbers of movers. But at the height of the dry season activity COLOSSYS was vital to a coherent and systematic effort designed to strike enemy trucks while they were still in the vicinity of a known location.[56/]

FERRET III. Another real time targeting aid introduced during
COMMANDO HUNT III was the 553d Reconnaissance Wing's (RW) FERRET III
program which began on 18 February 1970. This newest of the FERRET
operations was designed to provide real-time sensor-derived target
advisories[57/] and differed from previous versions by the installation
of X-T Plotters on the 553RW's EC-121Rs (call sign BATCAT). Before the
introduction of this device FERRET operations were conducted by airborne
operators who monitored sensor activations on manual sensor-display
stations known as Tell Tale displays. Vehicular or personnel targets
derived from this read out were passed to ABCCC with follow-on reports
to the ISC and 7th AF. The operator was required to keep manual logs
and had difficulty in monitoring more than five sensor fields
simultaneously.[58/]

Each X-T Plotter featured 99 electro-static metal "pins" which
were arranged horizontally so that a constantly revolving roll of paper
marked off in Greenwich Mean Time periods brushed against them (See
Figure 12 and 13). One pin represented a single (usually seismic)
sensor. All sensors in a particular string were assigned to contiguous
pins, with the northernmost sensor usually being on the left of the
group and the southernmost on the right. In practice, less than 99
sensors could be monitored on each plotter, since one pin was reserved
between every two strings to mark a line separating them. This was
necessary for clarity and to help the operator distinguish clearly between strings. Upon receiving a sensor activation, an electrical

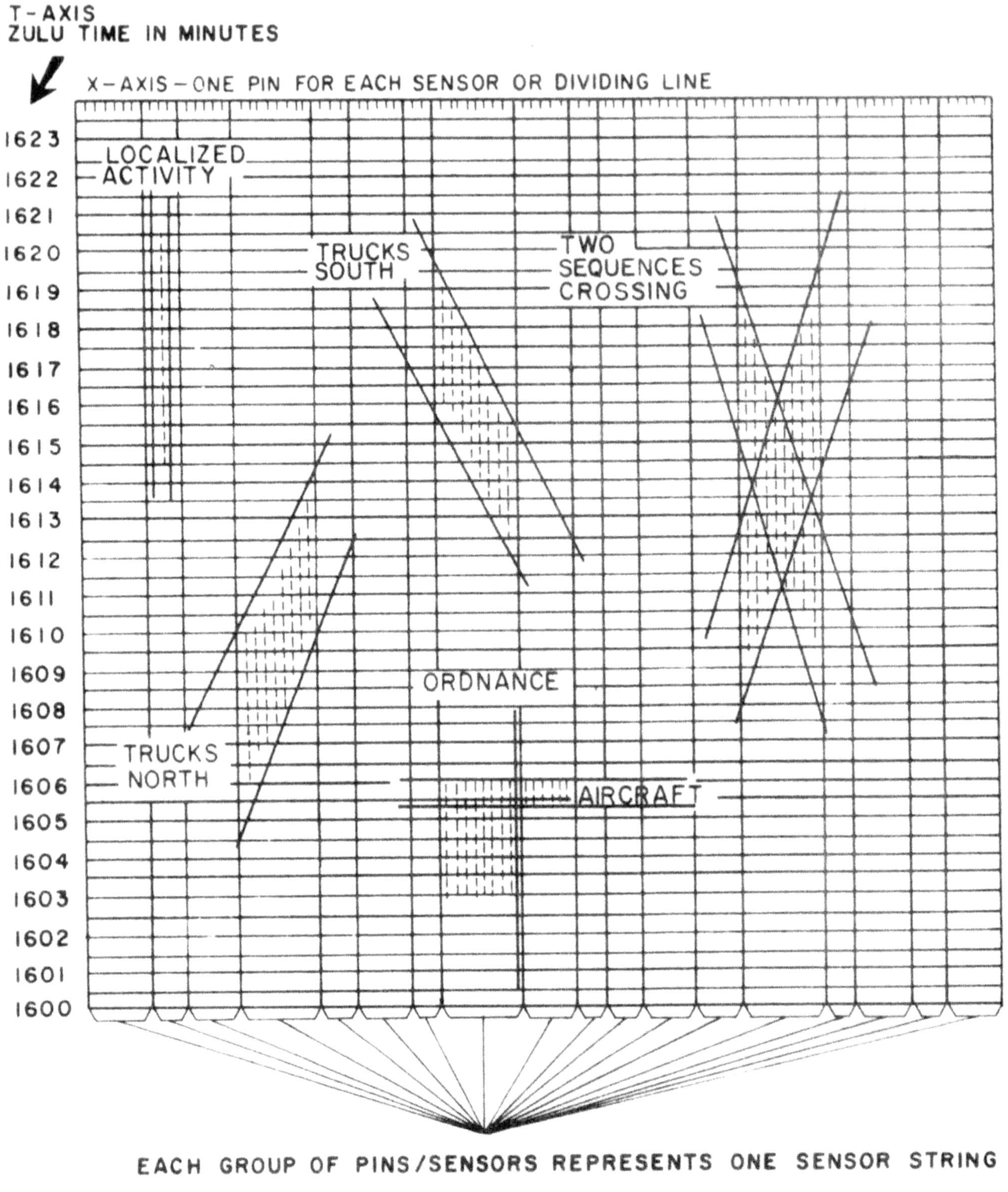

FIGURE 12

X-T Plotter Mounted aboard EC-121R BATCAT for FERRET III Operations.

FIGURE 13

charge which "burned" a short line in the paper was sent through the particular pin. While the CONFIRM sheets and console displays used by the GSM showed the total number of 10-second activations recorded by a sensor for any given period, the X-T Plotter displayed a separate mark for each activation. These marks were registered as they occurred, rather than being totalized and displayed after the end of the minute. In this sense, X-T Plotters gave information of a more "real time" nature than the ISC, although the lack of a computer and automatic relay of information required all operations to be conducted manually. Activations were interpreted into sequences and movers by means of patterns similar to those found on CONFIRM sheets. A limited audio assessment capability was present which aided in distinguishing movers from activations caused by wind, rain, aircraft, and hyper-active sensors. The lack of a Spectrum Analyzer, however, significantly limited FERRET III's ability to assess precisely the nature of the activations.[59]

BATCAT-mounted X-T Plotters were especially useful on Purple Orbit in extreme southern STEEL TIGER where distances were too great to relay sensor data to TFA for COMMANDO BOLT or advisory service action.[60] Sequences interpreted by the on-board GSM as representing movers were passed in a near-real time basis to FACs and gunships for strike action. Upon arrival on-station, FERRET III BATCATs would clear with ABCCC and then pass their advisories directly to strike aircraft operational frequencies. Upon completion of their on-station time, the EC-121R would again clear through ABCCC and obtain visually-reported results of FERRET III-initiated strikes from the FACs.[61]

From 1-15 May 1970 a special evaluation was conducted by TFA and the 553D RW to determine the relative effectiveness of FERRET III compared with the SPOTLIGHT program in which mover sequences were relayed from the ISC to ABCCC for strike action. SPOTLIGHT reports were passed to ABCCC only after the developing sequence had been entered into the computer by the GSM and had been determined to equal or exceed the minimum number of trucks (usually five) which ABCCC required before a sequence would be accepted. During the two week evaluation, SPOTLIGHT sequences were called to ABCCC an average of 13 minutes after the trucks began to exit the string. The test was conducted with both SPOTLIGHT and FERRET III monitoring the same 10 Blue Orbit strings. Results are depicted in Table 6. FERRET III calls were made to strike aircraft on a real time basis as a sequence was developing, while the time lag noted in SPOTLIGHT allowed the trucks to leave the vicinity of the sensors, take alternate routes, or pull into truck parks. During the evaluation, BATCAT assessed 1998 trucks against the ISC's 1946 on the same 10 Blue Orbit strings.[62]

The evaluation report cited the following factors as contributing to FERRET III success:[63]

    a. Real time operation.

    b. Ability of experienced personnel to distinguish between random activations and true truck sequences.

c. Ability of experienced personnel to determine numbers and direction.

d. Ability of BATCAT to monitor UHF strike frequency communications and determine if strike aircraft were available and free to accept the sequence.

TABLE 6

RESULTS OF EVALUATION OF SPOTLIGHT AND FERRET III
1-15 MAY 1970 [64]

	SPOTLIGHT	FERRET III
Number of Advisories Passed to FACs	22	341
Number of Trucks Passed to FACs	126	809
Number of Advisories Investigated	22	105
Number of Trucks Confirmed	-	133
Number of Trucks Struck	7	67
Number of Trucks Destroyed	0	12
Number of Trucks Damaged	0	11

An earlier study of FERRET III had identified two limitations: [65]

a. FACs and gunships were frequently engaged in strikes and could not be interrupted by further advisories.

b. Strike aircraft sometimes were operating at a distance from the area to which the sequence of advisory applied.

During discussions with TFA personnel, the effectiveness of FERRET III in detecting enemy activity was generally confirmed, but its ability to accurately distinguish random activations from truck sequences, and to determine numbers of movers was questioned. These deficiencies would be corrected in part by the addition to the system of a complete audio assessment capability (including a Spectrum Analyzer capability). The limited number of pins available for assignment to individual sensors also adversely affected the operation. This limit necessitated a trade-off between monitoring all sensors in fewer strings, or only certain sensors in a larger number of strings. One option limited the size of the areas that could be monitored, while the other restricted the amount of information available to assess the nature of the activation, and the direction, speed, and number of possible movers. 66/

COMMANDO HUNT IV (Apr - Oct 1970)

During the 1970 Southwest Monsoon, COMMANDO BOLT operations continued in the Ban Karai area. After the Mu Gia entry corridor closed down in March, COMMANDO BOLT operations were shifted south in response to enemy activity. With the concurrence of 7th AF, a third COMMANDO BOLT area was established in the Ban Raving area, west of the DMZ. Certain LOC monitoring strings along Routes 1036/1039 were lengthened and converted into COMMANDO BOLT strike strings on 25-26 April. Terrain masking problems affecting the lengthened strings required a slight relocation of Green Orbit for adequate monitoring. From 15 April to 15 June 802 COMMANDO BOLT sorties were flown in the Ban Karai area and another 101 in support of the Ban Raving program. 67/

A number of changes occurred at TFA during COMMANDO HUNT IV. Since the termination of SYCAMORE Control in April 1969, much of TFA's large Directorate of Operations (DO) had become superfluous. The subsequent emphasis on intelligence and targeting rather than operations activities finally resulted in the abolishment of DO on 30 June 1970. Certain important operational functions (such as the Sensor/Munitions Division and COMMANDO BOLT) were redistributed to the remaining directorates, Technical Operations (TO) and Intelligence (IN). 68/

The second major change implemented during this period involved the removal of one of TFA's two IBM 360/65 computers. This economy measure resulted in a loss of backup capability and a certain degree of flexibility. During the rest of COMMANDO HUNT IV and for subsequent campaigns, the remaining computer was used for real time read out and processing of sensor data for COMMANDO BOLT operations from later afternoon to around 0500 Laos time daily. The daylight time (approximately 11 hours) was used for data base and machine maintenance, as well as a variety of data processing functions. 69/ These two reductions resulted in the elimination of 155 military manning slots by 30 June 1970. 70/

COMMANDO HUNT V (Oct 1970 - Apr 1971)

Plans were prepared in August 1970 to increase the number of COMMANDO BOLT strings for COMMANDO HUNT V from the rainy season's six to approximately 20. 71/ At the same time, COMMANDO BOLT strike strings were lengthened from a maximum of six to a maximum of eight sensors apiece.⁷²/ Strike modules were composed of two or three of these strings, although exceptionally long strings of 18 sensors were used occasionally.⁷³/ This was to insure strings of adequate length to determine accurately truck speed and direction as well as allow TFA to continue monitoring the trucks until strike aircraft could arrive.⁷⁴/

COMMAND BOLT operations continued in the Ban Karai and Ban Raving areas as well as along Routes 920, 911 and 922. The performance of COMMANDO BOLT measured in terms of trucks destroyed and damaged per sortie varied greatly as the campaign proceeded and as the route became more and then less lucrative. This is depicted graphically in Figure 14.⁷⁵/ Since many attacks were conducted under non-visual conditions, inability to accurately assess target damage was a major factor in determining results.⁷⁶/

Airspace crowding problems similar to those which occurred in COMMANDO HUNT III's COMMANDO BOLT operations reappeared during COMMANDO HUNT V. It was difficult to conduct COMMANDO BOLT operations when gunships were in the same sector. On 6 March 1971 7th AF directed TFA to identify COMMANDO BOLT areas that would have the least interference with gunship operations. Gunships were the primary source of truck BDA and 7th AF was anxious to cover the most lucrative truck-hunting areas with these aircraft.⁷⁷/

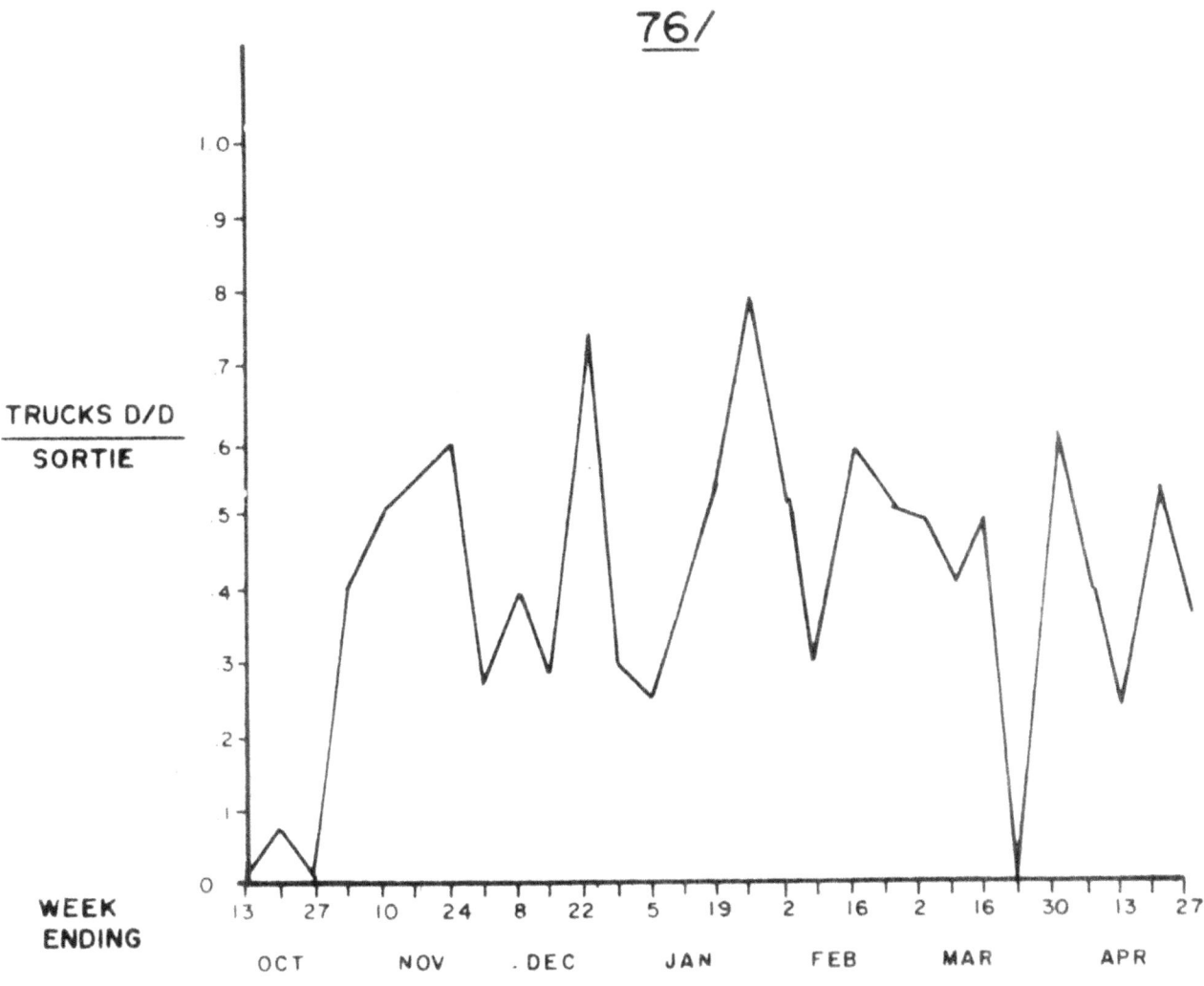

FIGURE 14

These circumstances definitely limited COMMANDO BOLT by reducing its number of strikes on movers, especially after gunship operations increased during January and March. COMMANDO BOLT aircraft occasionally were forced to expend on fixed targets when the presence of gunships prevented them from attacking targets passing through strike strings. At no time, however, were COMMANDO BOLT strike strings allowed to expire because gunships prevented their regular use.[78]

Partly as a result of conflicts with gunships, COMMANDO BOLT regularly began to strike fixed targets in STEEL TIGER. Many of these targets were identified by TFA's target development branch (INTT) through the Night Fixed Targeting Program. These new COMMANDO BOLT tactics required that the precise LORAN coordinates for the targets be determined so that they could be attacked under non-visual conditions by either offset bombing (COMMANDO NAIL) or LORAN (PAVE PHANTOM) techniques. Strike pilots followed procedures similar to those employed against moving targets with the only differences being that no course or speed adjustments had to be made to insure a specific TOT. COMMANDO BOLT fixed targets also were struck when weather prevented daytime visual strikes, or when no sequences occurred through strike modules upon which pre-fragged strike aircraft could expend ordnance.[79]

There were further indications during COMMANDO HUNT V that the enemy was monitoring US strike frequencies and using this information to adjust their truck movements. A 12 December 1970 message from TFA reported that truck movement had been observed to increase at the end of aircraft on-station time and decrease as aircraft would check in with COPPERHEAD. TFA requested that in the future aircraft report their "playtime" by means of secure voice communications or use encyphering methods for those transmissions broadcast in the clear.[80/]

Traffic Advisory Service. A Traffic Advisory Service for FACs and gunships and the newly arrived B-57G was introduced during COMMANDO HUNT V. This service was developed in an effort to make better use of sensor information in acquiring real time targets and as a replacement for the EC-121Rs of the FERRET III program. The EC-121R was scheduled to be replaced during the campaign by QU-22B monitor/relay aircraft which had no capabilities for on-board sensor read out.

The advisory service became operational on 24 October 1970[81/] and was based on the COLOSSYS computer program (See Figure 15). By use of the light pen, the GSM instantaneously transferred developing sequences to the advisory service controller (call sign HEADSHED) where it was displayed on his IBM 2260 console. The display contained the following information:[82/]

        a. Beginning time of sequence.

        b. VR sector and sensor string number.

        c. Size, type, direction and speed of mover(s).

        d. Time when advisory was displayed.

        e. Automatic Sequence Routing (ASR) number. (ASR was a computer process by which the above information was automatically relayed from TFA to ABCCC and 7th AF, and stored for eventual incorporation into the TFA data base).

HEADSHED Night Traffic Advisory Station in TFA Control Room.

FIGURE 15

Upon receipt of this information, the HEADSHED controller was able to communicate directly with strike aircraft by radio and alert them to the target in near-real time. This was just an advisory, however, and unlike COMMANDO BOLT, the strike aircraft still retained the option of ignoring the reported target if engaged in other activities or attacks. This operation also differed from COMMANDO BOLT in that advisories were passed to gunships as well as fighters, and attacks were made on a visual basis rather than according to LORAN coordinates. It was the responsibility of the strike aircraft to locate a strikeable target once HEADSHED had informed him of an area in which sensors indicated activity. By late December, 17 additional sensor strings had been emplaced specifically to support the Target Advisory Service.[83/]

Prior to initiation of this advisory service, this information had been passed as a SPOTLIGHT report to ABCCC for relay to strike aircraft. ABCCC, however, was limited in the manner of advisories it could control at one time, and TFA had been allowed to pass only sequences which contained a specified minimum number of movers (usually five). The new procedure removed this limitation and greatly increased the number of advisories passed.[84/] The instantaneous, automatic data relay between the GSM and HEADSHED made possible by COLOSSYS was also a great improvement over the telephone procedures used in SPOTLIGHT, and significantly reduced the time between target identification and notification of strike aircraft.[85/] Table 7 reflects TFA Target Advisory Service activity during the most active truck-killing months of COMMANDO HUNT V.

TABLE 7

TFA NIGHT TRAFFIC ADVISORY SERVICE SUMMARY [86/]

(HEADSHED)

JANUARY-APRIL 1971

SEQUENCES:

Number of Sequences Processed	69,723
Number of Sequences Passed	21,363

SEQUENCES PASSED TO:

COMMANDO BOLT	7,716
FACs	3,911
Gunships	4,863
Armed Recce	1,889
ABCCC	2,984
7AF Command Post	10

OPREP-4 REPORTED BDA RESULTED FROM ADVISORIES:

Trucks Destroyed	2,739
Trucks Damaged	586
Explosions	1,793
Fires	1,490

Phase III Sensors. Conversion of the IGLOO WHITE field to Phase III sensors was completed during COMMANDO HUNT V. Phase III sensors featured greater flexibility in assignment of monitoring frequencies and other advantages which are discussed in Chapter III. At the beginning of the campaign, 88 percent of the STEEL TIGER sensor field consisted of Phase III devices. The northernmost third of the field was entirely converted to Phase III by 1 October, the central by 1 November and the remainder by 17 February 1971.[87/]

Sensor String "Band" Concept. During previous interdiction campaigns LOC-monitor sensor strings had been located in a linear fashion along the roads of STEEL TIGER. This method of emplacement accurately recorded enemy vehicle traffic through a particular area since no known alternative routes existed. By COMMANDO HUNT V, however, the Laotian route structure had expanded and the great number of bypasses and alternate routes as well as ever-growing numbers of truck parks and storage areas allowed enemy truck traffic to avoid (often unknowingly) sensor strings and consequently not be included in the overall picture of traffic patterns. TFA awareness of this problem led to the "band" concept of sensor emplacement by which strings were placed on all possible routes, bypasses, and alternates in lines cutting across strategically located choke points, areas where routes converged, and across exit gates (See Figures 16 and 17). Any vehicles passing through a band would be detected by one sensor string and

COMMANDO HUNT V
SENSOR STRING DEPLOYMENT CONCEPTS

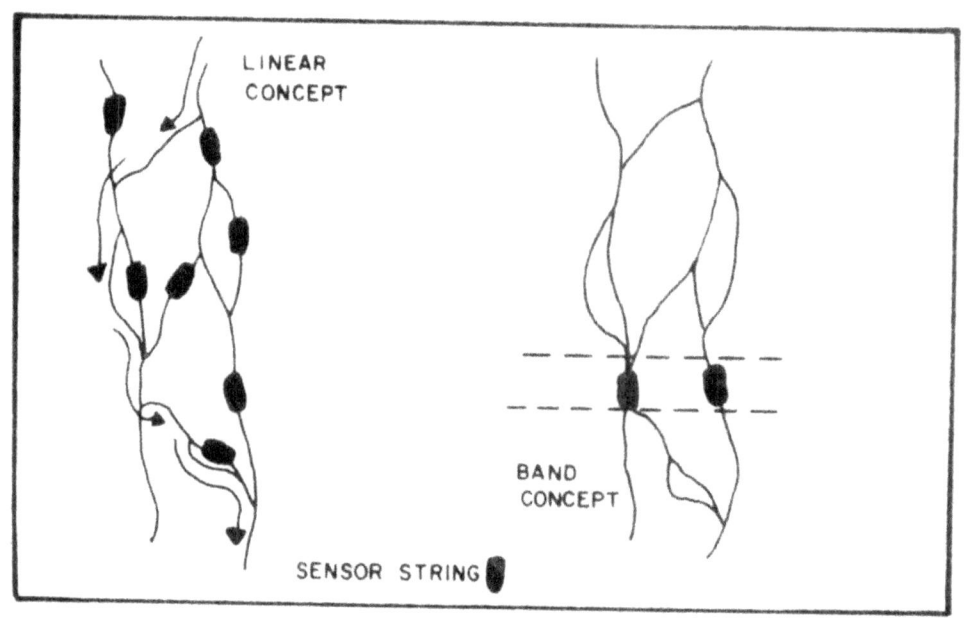

FIGURE 16

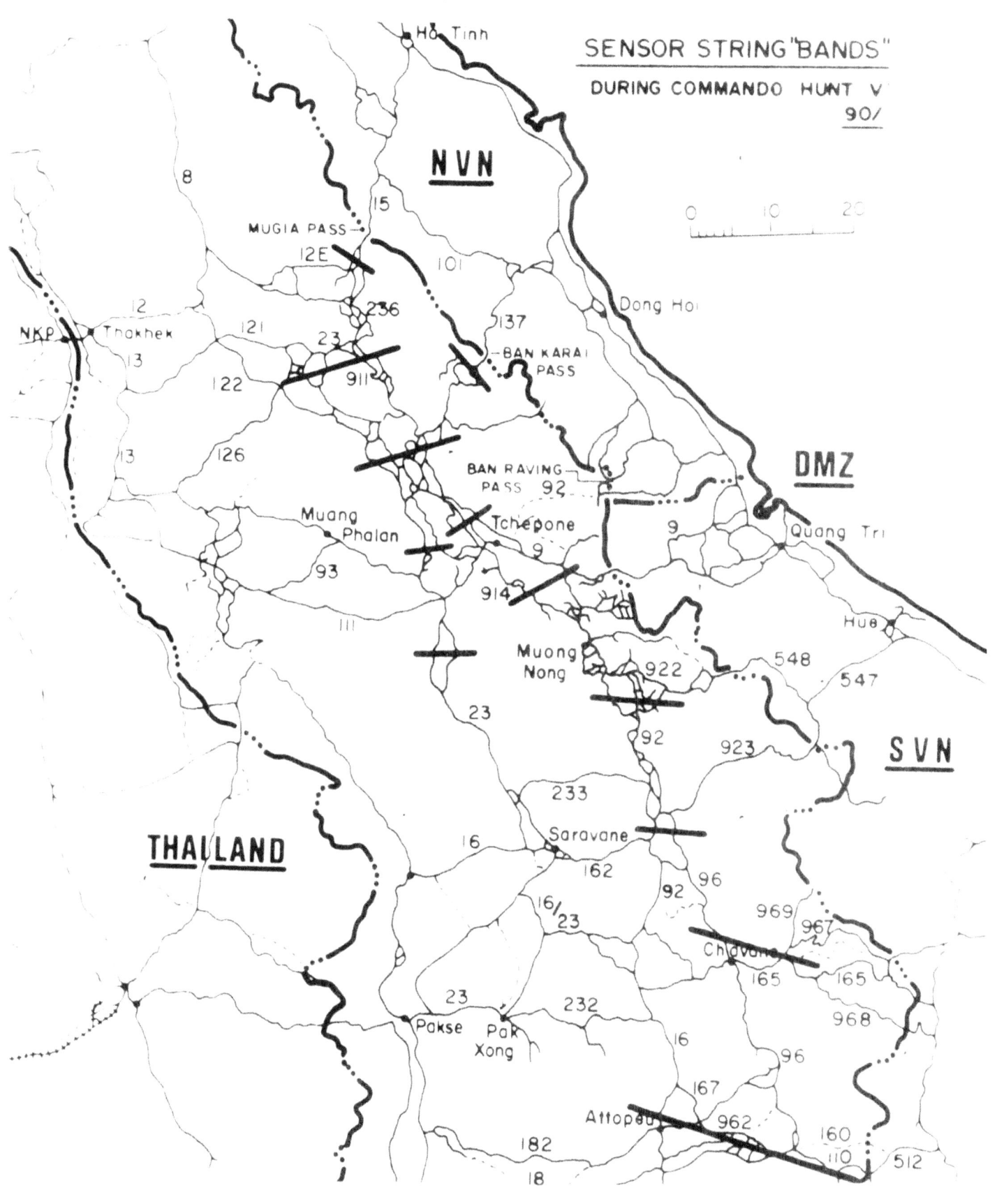

FIGURE 17

counted only on that string, regardless of the road used.[88] This configuration also sought to minimize double-counting of trucks.[89]

Night Fixed Targeting Program. On 5 January 1971, TFA initiated a night fixed targeting effort utilizing sensor-derived information. By analyzing sensor patterns and enemy truck movements, areas were singled out as possible locations of currently active targets such as truck parks, storage areas, or transshipment points. Based on UTM coordinates, a print out was obtained from the KEYWORD File giving all activity noted in the area for the past 30 days. This recent history of the target area was correlated with the sensor lead, and the targets officer selected a target based upon his analysis of the collated data. In many cases, recent film coverage or Special Intelligence (SI) data would also support target selection. When this process was complete, the target coordinates were passed to TFA strike controllers, 7th AF COC, the ABCCC or FACs for strike and/or prompt visual reconnaissance. COMMANDO BOLT aircraft were frequently used to deliver ordnance the following night. If collateral intelligence supporting the sensor-derived lead was insufficient, the lead was referred to FACs, PIs and targets personnel for further development.[90]

The night fixed targeting program differed from normal target development in that the leads were derived primarily from an analysis of sensor intelligence rather than from FAC, SI, or photographic information.

Lucrative leads from sensors could be quickly supported by other intelligence sources from the KEYWORD File and strike recommendations made the same night that the initial indication was received. Previous target development procedures required nominations to 7th AF by message and a lengthy process before the location was finally fragged and struck (normally three days for Tac Air and four days for Arc Light targets).[91/] This program supplemented rather than replaced the normal targeting process and was a further attempt to derive useful targets from IGLOO WHITE's ability to provide real time information on enemy activity.

Night-fixed targets were classed as "A" or "B" targets. "A" targets were those which were expected to be lucrative for less than 48 hours and required immediate strike action. Examples were certain truck parks and storage areas in use for only a short time. "B" targets were expected to remain lucrative for as long as 30 days. These latter were passed to the day targeters for further development, rather than immediate nomination and strike.[92/]

The night-fixed targeting program reported the following results for the period 5 January through 15 September 1971:[93/]

	NOMINATED	STRUCK	STRUCK WITH POSITIVE BDA
"A" Targets passed for strike within 48 hours	819	125	65
"B" Targets passed for further development	471	161	109

X-T Plotter. In late January 1971, the installation of an X-T Plotter was completed in the plot room at TFA. For the past year this device had been mounted in EC-121R sensor-monitor aircraft as the basis of the FERRET III program and had given these aircraft the ability to read out a selected set of up to 99 sensors per plotter. This capability allowed the EC-121Rs to send near-real time traffic advisories direct to FACs and gunships and performed many functions of an airborne ISC.[94/]

While this device greatly enhanced the EC-121R's capabilities, FERRET III experience had demonstrated that the computerized surveillance center at TFA was still superior to the X-T Plotter in detailed analysis:[95/]

> *Identification of sensor-detected movers by X-T Plotter readout is not as reliable as when accomplished by the computer-aided process used at TFA which includes greater audio and spectrum analysis validation capability. However, the X-T Plotter does provide read out in areas where relay of sensor data to TFA is not possible (extreme southern STEEL TIGER) and in other areas when the TFA computer is not on the line.*
>
> *. . .the X-T Plotter provides targets only in the sense that it identifies that movers are passing through a sensor string, and this information is used to provide traffic advisories to aircraft in near-real time. At very best it could pinpoint the location of a mover to within the detection range of a given sensor. Direction of movement is apparent, but speed of movement can be determined only approximately.*

TFA's X-T Plotter served as a backup when the computer was unavailable because of required maintenance or was engaged in data processing and analysis tasks. The X-T Plotter was also employed for periodic daylight monitoring of Green and Blue Orbits during March and April 1971, and for the round-the-clock monitoring of certain sensor strings in the Lam Son 719 area during that operation. Other roles for the plotter included an operator training function in conjunction with the computer in which comparisons of computer and plotter readouts for the same sensor strings produced excellent results. TFA's X-T Plotter read out the deployable Automatic Relay Terminal (DART I) field in northern RVN from 7-24 March 1971 when this system's read out facility was down for maintenance and again during July when the DART facility at Quang Tri was dismantled for transfer to TFA. The presence of the X-T Plotter also served to partially compensate for the removal of one of TFA's two IBM 360/65 computers.[96/]

Lam Son 719. The tight security precautions which characterized preparations for Lam Son 719 prevented the inclusion of a plan for the employment of IGLOO WHITE in the initial planning for the operation. Once the security hold was lifted, however, the Army implanted and read out sensor strings for security along Route 9 and around Khe Sanh.[97/] Marine OV-10s also emplaced 41 strings in the same areas in support of ground forces. During the withdrawal phase of the operation an additional 12 strings were emplaced by F-4s along Routes 9 and 925 and again around Khe Sanh.[98/] Sensors were credited with detecting 5232 targets,[99/] 694 of which were engaged by artillery, 14 by mortars and three by remotely-triggered mines. No BDA was recorded since the majority of the responses occurred at night or during inclement weather. There are no records of USAF sorties directed against sensor-derived targets because the target source was not specified in the mission reports.[100/]

As the operation progressed, the ARVN commander was notified of the availability of F-4 implanted sensor strings. Two route-monitor strings subsequently were requested and implanted. Advisors also emphasized to ARVN forces the opportunity to implant stay-behind sensors as friendly forces withdrew. ARVN commanders, however, were reluctant to become involved in emplacing these devices since equipment and teams familiar with implant techniques were not readily available. ARVN approval was finally given during the withdrawal phase of the operation, but it was by then too late to implement the plan.[101/]

The major lesson learned concerning the use of sensors during Lam Son 719 was that sensors can be used in an effective and timely manner in large ground operations only if they are incorporated into the operational planning from the beginning.[102/] The utilization of stay-behind sensors also requires careful advance planning so that the necessary equipment, skills and relay/read out capabilities are available. Terrain masking problems should also be examined beforehand.[103/]

COMMANDO HUNT VI (Apr - Oct 1971)

The COMMANDO HUNT VI rainy season plan reduced the maximum number of active sensor strings in STEEL TIGER from COMMANDO HUNT V's high of 128 [104] to 96. [105] After consultation with 7th Air Force, it was decided to begin the campaign with the maximum number of sensor strings and then eliminate strings as the enemy abandoned the routes they monitored. [106] Towards the end of the campaign, the total number had fallen to approximately 50. [107]

DART I Transfer. Of major importance to the future role of TFA was the transfer in early July of the Air Force-operated DART I sensor read out facility from Quang Tri, RVN, to TFA. The DART I system monitored sensor fields within northwestern RVN, including the Western Reconnaissance Zone (WRZ - western Quang Tri Province, RVN), the western Demilitarized Zone (DMA) and the A Shau Valley for the U.S. Army's XXIV Corps. The combination of DART I and IGLOO WHITE at one location was expected to provide a real time target correlation and strike capability against enemy forces infiltrating through the DMZ and along the Laos/RVN border. At the same time, the DART I data base was combined with TFA's. [108]

Additional Sensor Channels. Early planning for the COMMANDO HUNT VII campaign envisioned a sensor field substantially larger than that for COMMANDO HUNT V because of the anticipated expansion of IGLOO WHITE to LOCs in western STEEL TIGER. [109] With the 32

43

sensor channels then available for use, the maximum number of sensor strings possible consisted of approximately 150 strings. Requests by 7th AF in May resulted in eight additional channels being allocated to IGLOO WHITE, and a further eight being reserved for possible future use.[110/] Seventh Air Force expressed hopes in July that new transmitters would be available for installation in sensors during September, so the new channels could be utilized. With 40 channels available for sensor operations (including three allocated to DART I/XXIV Corps), the maximum number of strings (with seven sensors apiece) technically feasible rose to approximately 200.[111/] Plans to reduce the maximum number of sensors per string to four or five for COMMANDO HUNT VII would make a significantly larger number of strings possible.

COMPASS FLAG. Another important addition to TFA during COMMANDO HUNT VI was the COMPASS FLAG program. This was a Special Intelligence (SI) collection program which was expected to greatly improve TFA's effectiveness:[112/]

> *COMPASS FLAG affords TFA the opportunity for more timely fusion of SI data with that from sensors and other sources of information. Proximity of the COMPASS FLAG ground terminal to the ISC means that results of preliminary analysis of the COMPASS FLAG product by USAF Security Service (USAFSS) personnel will be readily available for TFA use. Conversely, reports on enemy activity based on sensor activations may enable USAFSS analysts to produce a more complete product from COMPASS FLAG collection.*

It should be kept in mind that COMPASS FLAG was not part of IGLOO WHITE but was established at TFA so the two programs could mutually support each other.

As originally conceived, the QU-22B aircraft was to have provided air support for COMPASS FLAG activities by flying a special mission over STEEL TIGER designated Yellow Orbit.[113/] QU-22B difficulties in August 1971, however, resulted in an evaluation of the C-130 as an alternate platform.[114/] Although hopes were expressed that IGLOO WHITE and COMPASS FLAG functions could be combined in the same aircraft, the 6908th Security Squadron (SS) at TFA pointed out that both programs were designed around different orbits neither of which could be altered without degrading one or the other mission. Another potential problem was the desire to perform both functions by means of C-130s flying ABCCC missions. The 6908SS feared that communications transmissions necessary to the ABCCC would interfere seriously with COMPASS FLAG.[115/]

Reactivation of DO. Most significant of all for the future of TFA was the reactivation on 22 May 1971 of a Directorate for Operations (DO).[116/] This office had been deleted during COMMANDO HUNT II after SYCAMORE Control had been abolished and the direct control of strike aircraft operating over STEEL TIGER removed from TFA. The development and steady expansion of the COMMANDO BOLT system, the initiation of the Night Traffic Advisory Service and the move of DART I to the ISC resulted in TFA acquiring increased responsibilities in the operational sphere. Consequently, a central office was needed to effectively control and coordinate the efforts of these different functions.

A further indication of this increased operational orientation was the decision in late June to make TFA predominately a night operation. Instead of the former practice of operating the ISC on the basis of three roughly equal shifts daily, the majority of TFA's personnel were placed on a 1700 to 0500 work schedule to match the daily period of peak enemy activity. Skeleton crews remained on duty during the day to perform such functions as computer off-line operations, round-the-clock DART I monitoring and certain analysis functions.[117/] Although this new schedule was modified as enemy activity declined for the rainy season, the precedent had been set for subsequent dry season campaigns.

Use of IGLOO WHITE Outside of STEEL TIGER and South Vietnam

Cambodia. The involvement of Cambodia in hostilities against Communist forces opened this country for the first time to the possible employment of IGLOO WHITE sensors. A 19 May 1970 message from 7th AF Directorate of Targets Intelligence to TFA reported "considerable high level interest in the future need for sensor string coverage in northeastern Cambodia."[118/] A proposed area of interest was specified and TFA was instructed to determine the feasibility of such a Cambodian sensor field and the requirements for a read out orbit.[119/] On 5 June 1970, a Hq 7AF staff paper discussed guidance from Military Assistance Command Vietnam (MACV) Directorate of Special Operations (JE-04) concerning sensor operations in Cambodia:[120/]

    a. U.S. forces would be out of Cambodia by 30 June 1970.

    b. There would be no U.S. artillery firings across the border from the RVN after 30 June unless targets are definitely lucrative and firings are approved by Hq MACV (J-3).

    c. Sensors left in Cambodia by U.S. forces were for intelligence purposes only.

    d. Status of RVN forces in Cambodia after 30 June was unknown at that time.

The staff paper went on to review the approximately 170 stay-behind sensors emplaced by the 25th Infantry Division and the 1st Cavalry Division. These were all capable of being read out from relay points situated on mountains within the RVN (Nui Ba Den and Nui Ba Ra) as part of the Army's Battlefield Area Surveillance System (BASS) facilities. Also discussed was the need to relocate Orange Orbit if 7th AF assumed responsibility for monitoring Cambodian sensor fields and the impact this would have on existing IGLOO WHITE and DART requirements.[121/]

By 24 June, TFA decided that a sensor field of 20 strings would satisfy the minimum requirements of the coverage desired. Maps had been obtained and special photography to assist sensor implant planning was on order. A review of the Cambodian project, however, mentioned two difficulties: TFA had always been responsible for Laotian LOCs, and prior to the Allied incursion into Cambodia had no information concerning that country's route structure. The second and most difficult problem related to the fluid ground situation: FACs flying over Cambodia reported difficulties in distinguishing civilian from military traffic and friendly military from enemy military traffic. If these problems were not resolved it would be difficult to successfully apply IGLOO WHITE to Cambodia. The study also reported that the projected 20 string Cambodian sensor field would require two new read out orbits, since neither Purple nor Orange Orbits could be moved without serious detriment to IGLOO WHITE coverage of Southern Laos or the RVN.[122/] By 30 July, the proposed field had been expanded to 25 strings, but plans for actual implementation of the sensor implants had been put "on the shelf" at 7th AF.[123/]

On 27 September 1970, 7th AF directed that three sensor strings be implanted in northeastern Cambodia along Routes 13, 136, and 94 in hopes that they would detect an anticipated increase in enemy traffic from southern Laos into Cambodia.[124/] The three strings were implanted on 3 and 4 October and two-three hours of Purple Orbit were diverted each day to monitor them.[125/] These strings were monitored for a total of 36 hours from 4-16 October on a random basis, with one mover being detected along Route 13 on the night of 12 October. From these results, 7th AF concluded that the enemy was not moving vehicle traffic at night along the three routes.[126/] In conjunction with this evaluation, 7th AF also indicated its desire to retain the FERRET III EC-121Rs as long as possible in any phase down of these aircraft, in order that X-T Plotters could provide real time traffic advisories to strike aircraft if the full Cambodian contingency plan were ever implemented.[127/]

By the end of October, 7th AF Directorate of Targets Intelligence had decided that the objectives of a sensor field in northeastern Cambodia would be to "monitor the input routes from southern Laos into Cambodia and to monitor the throughput routes from southern Laos into southern MR III."[128/] Since the October test had been designed to monitor the

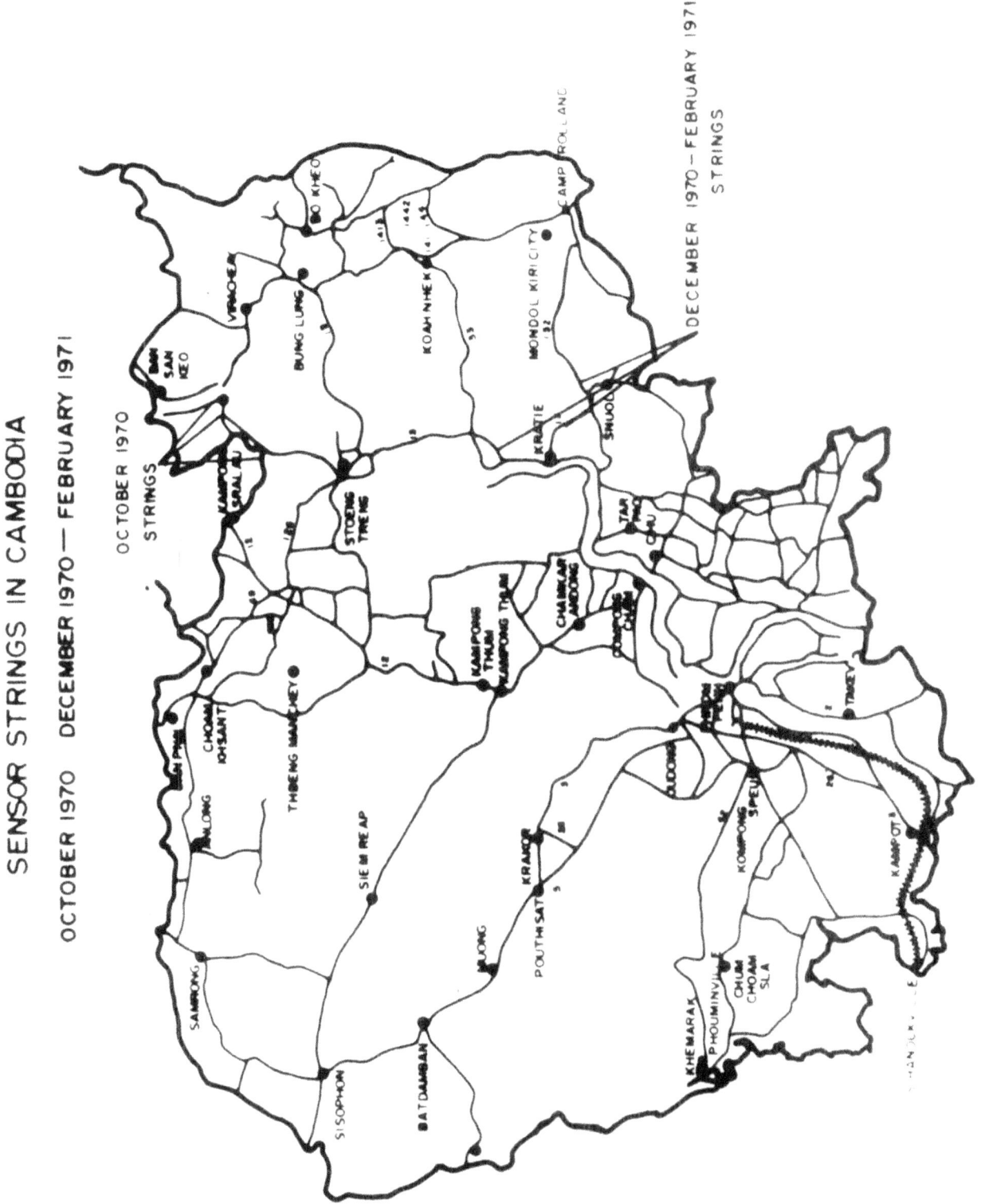

FIGURE 18

input routes, a second set of three sensor strings was implanted on 20 December along potential throughput Routes 13 and 132 in Cambodia.[129]

Unlike the strings in October, these sensors were Army devices which were hand-implanted by Vietnamese Air Force (VNAF) helicopter-borne personnel in areas where significant traffic had been observed. The orbit of the Tactical Air Control Center (TACC) EC-121R (TACC-A, or Black Orbit) was modified to permit monitoring of these strings, which continued from 21 December to 7 February.[130] During this time, two movers were detected on 24 December, one mover on 4 January and 11 on 14 January. A traffic advisory on one of the 24 December movers was passed to an AC-119G SHADOW gunship, but no results were reported. After the expiration of the sensor life spans, MACV felt that it was unlikely that a continuing sensor capability in that area would be worth the effort needed to monitor it effectively. It was recommended that if additional strings were desired, they should be placed on Routes 110A and 166B in southern Laos in order to detect traffic moving into Cambodia.[131]

BARREL ROLL. Sensor strings were first employed in BARREL ROLL (Northern Laos) in August 1969 to determine enemy traffic patterns and levels during a critical ground campaign. A special Rose Orbit had been established to monitor the strings by manual read out. Additional sensors were utilized along Route 7 in October and November,[132] but the changing situation made their continued employment unnecessary, and Rose Orbit was terminated on 24 January 1970.[133]

In August 1971, the 7th AF Deputy Chief of Staff for Operations commented on the possibility of the BARREL ROLL Airborne Command and Control Center (ABCCC) C-130E performing a role similar to that successfully undertaken by its STEEL TIGER counterpart and monitoring a sensor field on Route 7 east of Ban Ban. An investigation by TFA of terrain masking problems and enemy threat to the monitor-relay aircraft determined that a favorable orbit with minimal risk could be established, although certain sections of the route would have to be monitored from a second orbit that would expose the aircraft to a certain degree of risk from AAA, MIGs, and Surface-to-Air Missiles (SAMs) fired from within North Vietnam.[134/] Since no read out would be possible aboard the relay aircraft, the data would have to be transmitted to TFA for interpretation. It was proposed to use the recently installed DART antenna and receiver for this purpose if the need ever arose, since all other equipment was required to support IGLOO WHITE and COMPASS FLAG.[135/] No decision was made to proceed with a BARREL ROLL sensor field at that time.

North Vietnam. Another area for which the employment of IGLOO WHITE sensors was considered briefly was North Vietnam. Intelligence reports in late 1970 had indicated the deployment of four SAM Firing Battalions into the North Vietnamese panhandle south of 18° north latitude, probably to attack USAF aircraft operating against Laotian LOCs near North Vietnam's border. Since none of the Firing Battalions had been located, 7th AF intelligence on 7 December requested a study to determine the feasibility of placing sensors on LOCs along which SAMs would have to be moved to reach convenient firing positions. Since

SAM units were believed to require seven or eight hours to prepare for action after occupying a firing position, sensor detection of their movement into position would give sufficient warning of the impending attack to allow aircrews to be alerted. The request suggested that electrical engine ignition signatures might be useful in differentiating SAM equipment from other vehicles.[136/] A 15 December message from the Commander, U.S. Military Assistance Command, Vietnam (COMUSMACV) commented on this feasibility study (then being conducted at TFA) and indicated that if the study were favorable a request would be prepared asking for authority for sensor implants in North Vietnam.[137/]

TFA concluded that the project was not feasible with current equipment and knowledge. Seismic sensors were unable to distinguish between different vehicles, while acoustic sensors were limited by the ability to differentiate only tracked from wheeled vehicles. Another problem was that the enemy would still be able to move SAM equipment at times when the ISC was not in operation. Sensors in North Vietnam would have to be read out by Green Orbit; a move toward North Vietnam would place the aircraft beyond the MIG Combat Air Patrol (CAP) line, while a more secure location would significantly degrade Green Orbit's ability to perform its primary mission of monitoring sensors in the Ban Karai and Ban Raving areas.[138/]

CHAPTER III

SENSORS, SENSOR-RELATED DEVICES AND SPECIAL USES

By February 1971, the last Phase I and II sensors had been retired from the IGLOO WHITE Program and entirely superseded by Phase III types. Phase I sensors consisted primarily of the Navy's SONABUOY and Air Delivered Seismic Intrusion Detectors (ADSID). The former had only an audio capability, while the latter was solely a seismic sensor. The SONABUOY was available in two versions: the CANOPY ACOUBUOY which was designed to hang in the upper layers of the jungle canopy, and the SPIKE ACOUBUOY (SPIKEBUOY) which implanted in the ground. Two other Phase I sensors used in small numbers were the Helicopter Emplaced Seismic Intrusion Detector (HELOSID) and the Hand Emplaced Seismic Intrusion Detector (HANDSID). None of these sensors were commandable, and they broadcast on 31 channels, each with 27 distinct addresses. [139]

Phase II differed from Phase I sensors primarily in their commandability, especially the ability to command audio. These sensors could be instructed to send audio, go nonreal time (count impulses and store this information for later transmission on command), go real time (transmit impulses as they occur), and read out (transmit accumulated nonreal time impulses). ACOUBUOY and SPIKEBUOY sensors were converted to a Phase II mode, while the ADSID I was replaced by the Fighter Air Delivered Seismic Intrusion Detector (FADSID II). In addition, a combined seismic/acoustic sensor was delivered - the Acoustic-Seismic Intrusion Detector (ACOUSID II). High

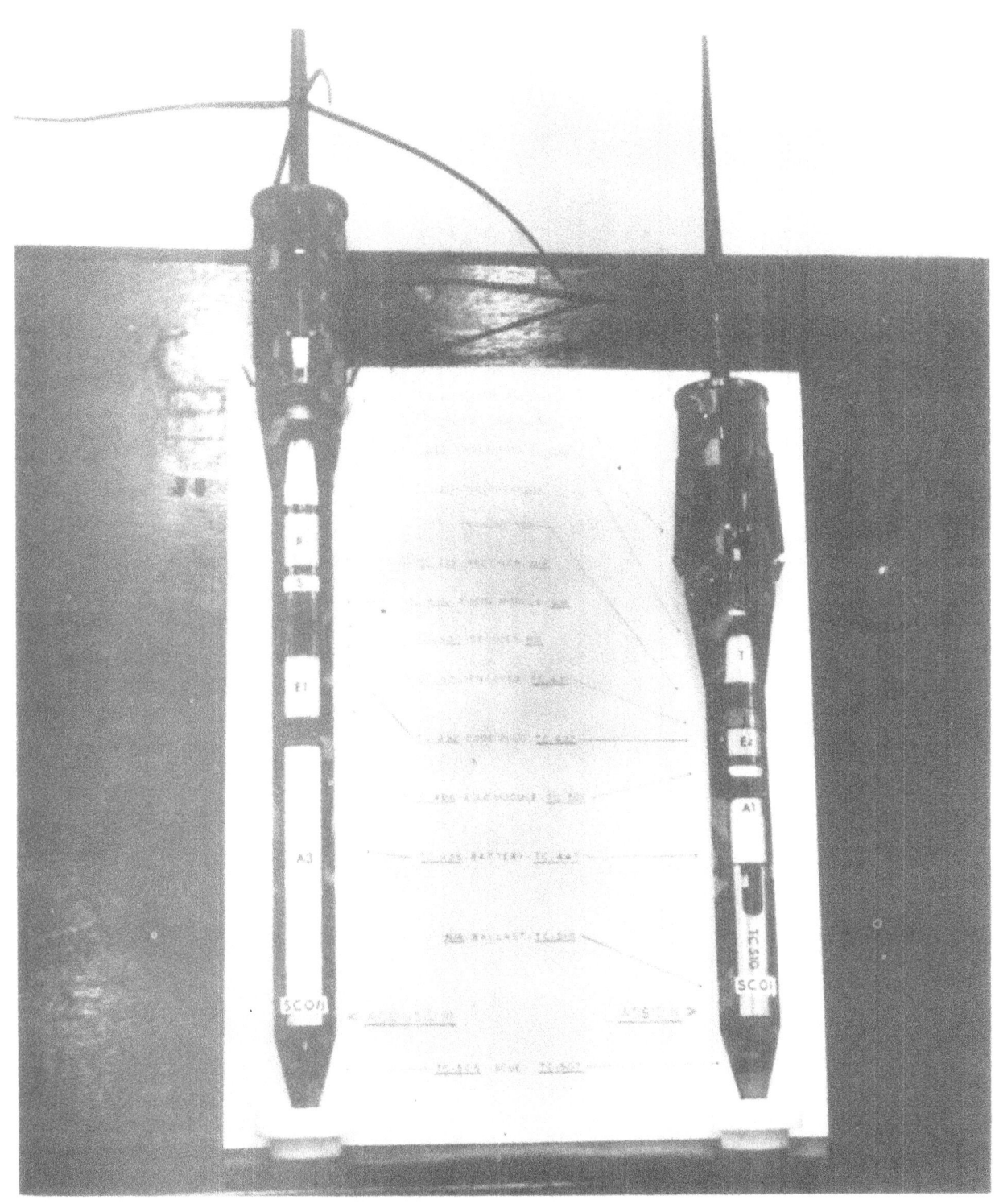

Phase III Sensors: Left, ACOUSID III
(4' long x 5" Maximum Diameter)
Right, ADSID III
(3' long x 5" Maximum Diameter)
Figure 19.

implant mortality rates for the FADSID II, however, resulted in the continued use of ADSID Is.[140/] A modified SPIKEBUOY called SPIKE Seismic Intrusion Detector (SPIKESID) was used in early 1970 on a test basis. This sensor was commandable and incorporated a seismic detection circuit and a field-selectable option which made SPIKESID acoustic or seismic or both.[141/]

Phase III sensors incorporated the commandable features of their predecessors, but increased the number of channels available to 32, with 64 sensor addresses each (instead of the previous 27).[142/] The use of common components in Phase III devices reduced costs and logistics complexities and allowed sensors to be tailored to specific situations.[143/] Sensors included Phase III versions of the ground implanted ADSID and ACOUSID, as well as the Commandable Microphone (COMMIKE III), which was suspended from jungle canopy.[144/]

Engine Detection Sensor (EDET III)

EDET III was an engine-detector sensor designed to detect pulsed radio frequency energy from the unshielded system of gasoline-powered engines.[145/] EDET electronic components were enclosed in standard COMMIKE III cases, restricting their use only to areas with sufficient jungle canopy to permit them to hang up. During an operational evaluation of the new sensor carried out by TFA from 27 March to 3 June 1971, 44 EDET IIIs were emplaced over existing, reliable ADSID/ACOUSID and COMMIKE strings to provide maximum verification of EDET III activations. As an LOC monitor, approximately 80 percent of the activations recorded during this test

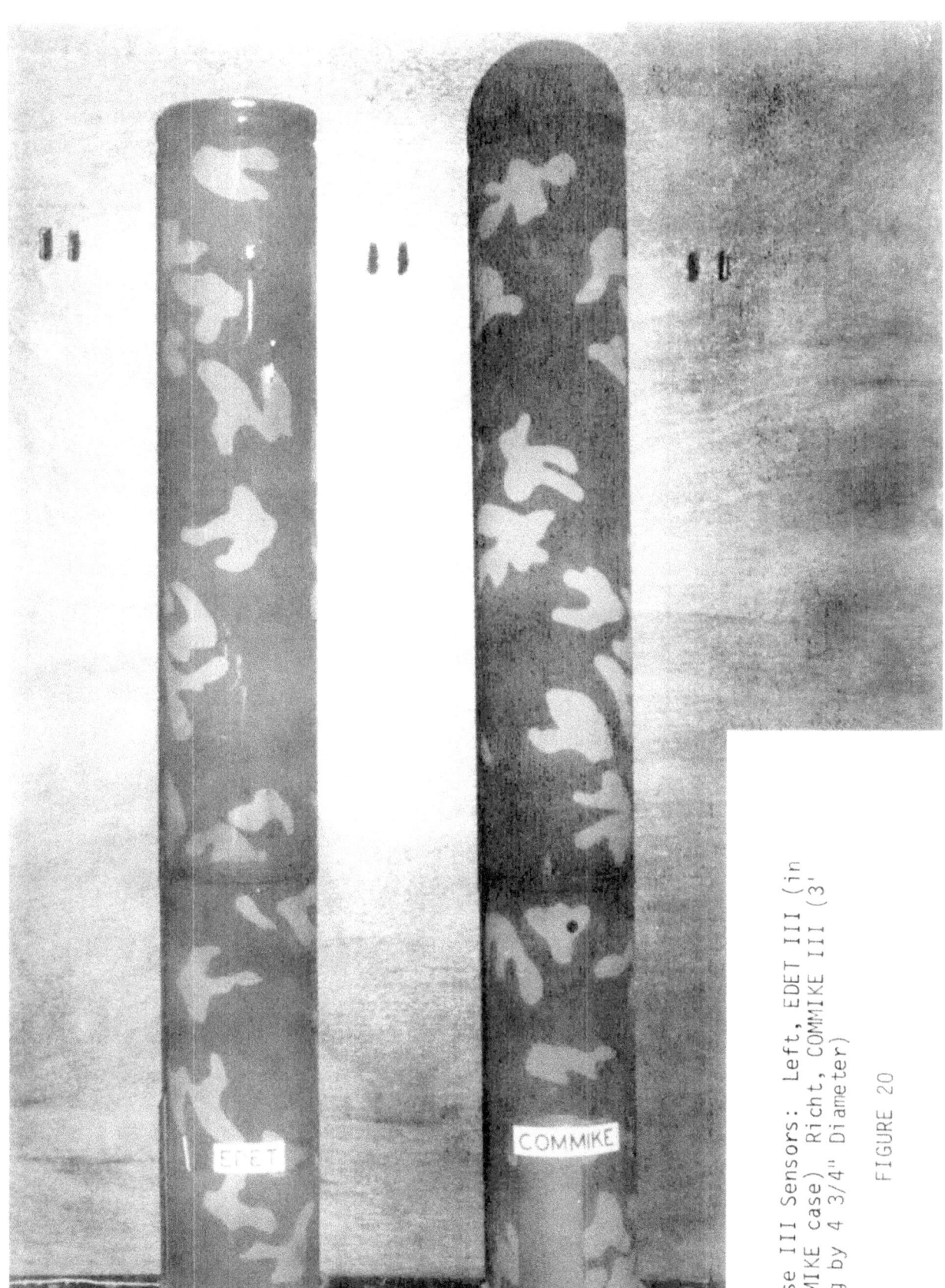

Phase III Sensors: Left, EDET III (in COMMIKE case) Richt, COMMIKE III (3' long by 4 3/4" Diameter)

FIGURE 20

correlated directly with ADSID/ACOUSID sequences. An additional 12 percent of the sequences not detected by EDET III indicated the presence of diesel powered vehicles, demonstrating EDET's indirect capability to differentiate between different power plants.* The remaining eight percent were attributed to false alarms from weather and lightning.[146/]

EDETs were partially successful as truck park monitors, especially when emplaced in conjunction with COMMIKEs. Like seismic sensors, EDETs responded automatically to an activation which was then displayed on the GSM's IBM 2250 display console. By polling COMMIKEs collocated with EDETs only when the EDET indicated activity, the acoustic sensors confirmed the presence of trucks 50 percent of the time. The standard TFA procedure was to poll COMMIKEs at random, a method which had only a six percent rate of truck detections. Per unit of time expended by the audio technician, the COMMIKE/EDET combination produced approximately eight times greater truck identification than the COMMIKE alone, and required only one-fifth the time. A combined COMMIKE/EDET system allowed a field to be monitored which was four to five times the size of one in which COMMIKEs were polled randomly. Lightning-produced false alarms were believed to have interferred occasionally with EDET truck identification, but the total number of such activations was considered much less than for ADSID/ACOUSID sensors because of the EDET's selective nature.[147/]

---

* EDETs cannot detect diesel-powered vehicles--can only detect the ignition of gasoline-powered vehicles.

On 13 May 1971, TFA reported that EDETs when used in conjunction with other sensors would be most useful for truck park monitoring and for detecting special purpose vehicles such as tanks, caterpillar tractors, and those with diesel engines. TFA also considered it to be less useful as an LOC monitor in dense jungle areas;[148/] earlier tests at Eglin Air Force Base, Florida, had indicated that the EDET's detection range decreased rapidly as jungle density increased.[149/]

Although the utility of the EDET III had been proven operationally, the extent of its use during COMMANDO HUNT VII was uncertain at the time of this report. In May 1971, TFA had stated that approximately 826 EDETs would be used during the coming campaign if the first could be made available by October 1971.[150/] By mid-August, CINCPACAF had authorized Air Force Systems Command (AFSC) to begin price negotiations for the procurement of 400 EDT IIIs, with initial delivery to be on or before 1 February 1972. Delivery rate was specified at between 20 and 35 per week.[151/]

In early August 1971, the Saigon office of the Defense Special Projects Group (DSPG) responsible for the overall development of IGLOO WHITE and formerly known as the Defense Communications Planning Group reported to its Washington office that motorized sampan traffic in the Mekong Delta area of the RVN had increased significantly and inquired as to the suitability of EDET IIIs to monitor this traffic.[152/] DSPG replied that the use of EDETs was feasible for this purpose as long as the rpm of the sampan's engine was high enough.[153/] Possibly as an outgrowth of this exchange was a TFA plan of mid-September to emplace a string of EDETs (with one COMMIKE) along the Se Kong River in southern STEEL TIGER south of Attopeu in an effort to detect motorized waterway traffic. This was a test plan only, with EDETs being obtained from stocks remaining after the March to June evaluation.154/

Commandable Audio-Engine Detector (CAEDET)

During the March to June tests EDET III modules were enclosed and emplaced in standard COMMIKE cases. Consequently, they were usable only in areas of heavy canopy. Additionally, the evaluation demonstrated that the effectiveness of the EDET/COMMIKE combination could be limited because the sensors had to be delivered in separate cases. If delivery conditions resulted in excessive distances between the final locations of the sensors, valid audio assessments and correlations between the two were impossible.155/

Bearing in mind these factors, TFA in June 1971 raised the possibility of combining EDET and COMMIKE components/capabilities in the same case. Also mentioned was the development of an EDET sensor either with an implant capability, or as part of existing seismic sensors. If successfully developed, EDETs could be delivered in either a ground-implant or tree hang-up mode and paired with audio or seismic capabilities with no danger of delivery dispersion limiting the effectiveness of the string.156/ Combined sensors would also reduce the number of delivery sorties required and allow strings of only two or three sensors to be used effectively.157/

TFA identified two significant deficiencies in current operational capabilities which sensors combining EDET, seismic, and acoustic characteristics would help correct. First, the enemy was increasing his use of diesel-powered tracked vehicles (tanks, bulldozers) and prime movers in Laos, but TFA was unable to distinguish these from those using conventional gasoline engines. Second, TFA could not adequately monitor the vast numbers of truck park/storage areas in use (or suspected use) by the enemy, or correctly determine the most lucrative time for strikes. [158/]

In July 1971, the Chief of Staff of the Air Force (CSAF) applied the term CAEDET to the proposed ignition/commandable acoustic sensor to prevent confusion with EDET III. [159/] Electronics Systems Division at Hanscom Field, Massachusetts, directed in August that the audio-ignition detection components would be designed to fit inside a container suitable for both a canopy hang-up and ground-implant role, [160/] but delivery of sensors was not believed possible before October 1972. [161/] As of the cut off date of this report, there were no firm plans to proceed with the development of an EDET combined with seismic capabilities.

Radar Beacon Transponder (RABET II)

Not all new sensor devices and applications were successful. One notable failure was the RABET II. This consisted of a 400 watt X-Band radar beacon enclosed in an ACOUSID II case which was implanted by an F-4. The beacon was designed as a target reference marker to aid radar bombing. When interrogated by an X-Band radar, the RABET II was supposed to transmit a response indicating its position.[162] Of six RABET II beacons test-dropped from July to October 1970, only one established contact after impact, and then only for seven or eight minutes.[163] These umpromising results led to the project's cancellation by the DCPG (now DSPG) on 24 December 1970.[164]

Acoustical Targeting

At the end of COMMANDO HUNT III, considerable doubt existed at TFA concerning the value of acoustic sensors. The presence of these sensors in LOC monitoring strings was regarded at that time as adding only insignificantly to the ability to define sequences, since three or four reliable seismic devices were believed adequate to confirm the presence of truck traffic. An acoustic capability was seen as useful only in certain special cases, such as with strings giving inadequate patterns because of ambiguity, high false alarm rates, or weak responses. Acoustic sensors were also useful at either end of COMMANDO BOLT strings to provide the maximum possible warning of approaching trucks, since acoustic detection range was approximately three times that of seismic.[165]

Acoustic sensors were considered of little value for area reconnaissance or monitoring purposes as well. From September 1968 to September 1969, 22 Reconnaissance by Acoustic (RBA) and "Occupational" (to determine enemy occupancy of an area)[166] sensor strings were in use in STEEL TIGER, but this had fallen to 16 for COMMANDO HUNT III.

One argument against RBA stressed the relative inefficiency of the RBA method as producers of target intelligence:[167]

> *In general, by the time we go through the effort of determining by photo and visual reconnaissance whether an area would be a likely site for an RBA string, we will already know whether or not there is a target warranting strike in the area. Knowing that, there is little use in emplacing the RBA string which was intended to answer the same question.*

Other problems concerned the dispersed nature of enemy storage facilities which meant that even well-placed acoustic strings usually sensed only low levels of activity even in major complexes. RBA emplacement sorties were also difficult to obtain, since LOC monitoring strings had a higher priority.[168]

A fresh look was taken at the value of acoustic targeting during COMMANDO HUNT V. In February 1971, an RBA program was initiated using COMMIKE IIIs to ascertain enemy activity in certain enemy truck park/storage areas covered by heavy canopy. A total of 11 COMMIKE strings were implanted in areas identified as potentially lucrative by evaluation of sensor patterns and inputs from all intelligence sources. Several targets were developed from this effort. In March, EDET IIIs were combined with the COMMIKEs as part of the evaluation of the new engine ignition detectors.[169]

In July 1971, TFA inaugurated the concept of Acoustic Targeting Areas (ATA). Under this concept acoustic intelligence gathering and analysis were done in terms of an area, which was monitored by a series of strings of two or three sensors each. Previously, RBA strings had averaged nine sensors each [170] and had functioned primarily as an intelligence collector. When RBA sensors had indicated enemy activity in an area, visual and photographic reconnaissance were used to determine a set of strike coordinates. ATAs went beyond this concept in that strikes could be called in on the basis of acoustic indications alone. [171] As of July 1971, 27 ATAs had been implanted, 40 assessments had been made in 16 of the areas, and two strikes called in with unknown results. [172]

The reemphasis of TFA from its previous role of an intelligence gatherer to that of a target developer accounted for much of the fresh attention devoted to acoustic targeting. Sorties were now available for acoustic sensor implants, since greater importance was being attached to programs with BDA potential, rather than those intended to count trucks or monitor LOCs. TFA was also considering a plan for COMMANDO HUNT VII to implant acoustic sensors in areas of heavy canopy in grid patterns, rather than the straight lines used in the past. [173]

Use of Sensors for Assessing BDA

Sensors were used for determining BDA only to a limited extent. An April 1971 7th AF report pointed out that for any damage assessment to be made, the vehicles would have to be within the string at the time of the attack, and the attack coordinated with TFA. Although this was possible with COMMANDO BOLT operations, it would be extremely difficult with other fighters or gunships, especially since only 3.5 percent of the motorable Laotian route structure was covered by sensor strings.[174]

Sensors often recorded activations immediately following strikes, but it was difficult to determine precisely if these were caused by exploding ordnance, secondary explosions, or enemy activity. Detection of a significant amount of continuing activity after conclusion of a strike would indicate an enemy presence in the area and a response to the attack. This could be the basis for a recommendation that the target be restruck. Although sensor (especially acoustic) BDA was a factor which was taken into account by TFA, it was never considered quantifiable or capable of being entered into the TFA data base as confirmed BDA.[175]

Portatale

In January 1970, a 10-day test/evaluation program was conducted by three OV-10s of the 23d Tactical Air Support Squadron (TASS) at Nakhon Phanom Royal Thai Air Force Base, Thailand (NKP), to determine the feasibility of adopting Portatale I Very High Frequency (VHF) receivers as an airborne aid to enable FAC aircraft to receive and display signals directs from IGLOO WHITE sensors in areas where terrain conditions masked read out by conventional monitoring and relay procedures.[176] The Portatale was a light weight, portable device which had the capability of decoding and displaying signals from sensors on any of 31 channels, one at a time (See Figure 21). Marine OV-10 crews at Da Nang had been using the device for this purpose and reported it to be simple in

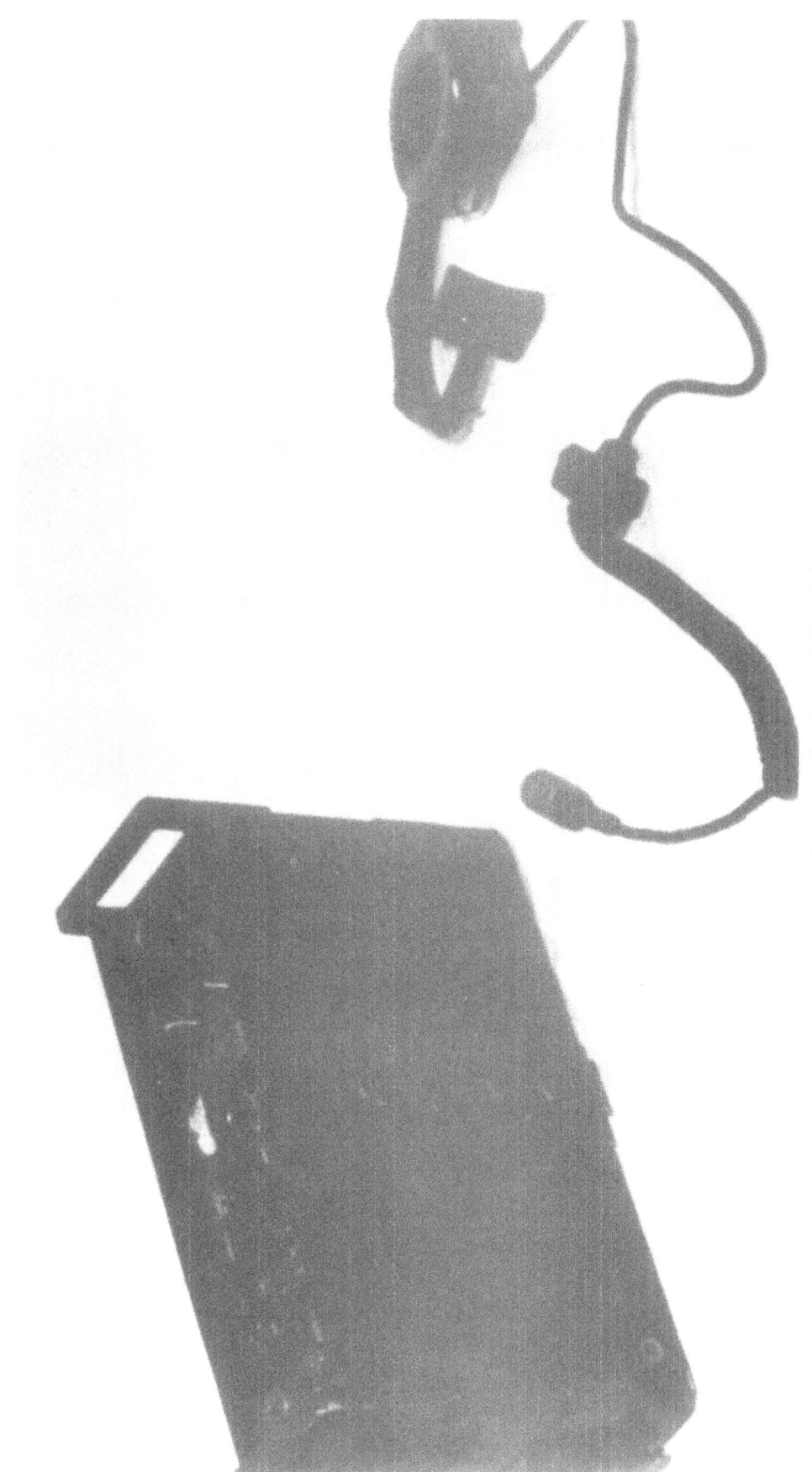

Portatale I and Headphone

FIGURE 21

operation and highly reliable. During the evaluation FACs of the 23TASS hoped to be able to conduct strikes on sensor-detected targets on a near-real time basis in areas where the use of sensors had previously been restricted, such as Rat Fink Valley and the Ban Laboy Fords, both near Ban Karai Pass. 177/

In early January 1970, the Director of Materiel Management at Kelly Air Force Base, Texas, authorized the implementation of a Class IB modification to equip Air Force OV-10s with Portatales in accordance with Naval Air Systems directives and guidance. 178/ This was accomplished by Air Force Personnel at NKP assisted by advisors from the III Marine Air Wing (MAW). 179/ In addition, two special strike strings consisting of four ADSIDs and one SPIKESID apiece were emplaced for the operation on 12 January in the Delta 57 area in Laos near the Xe Bang Fai River. 180/ Deteriorating weather and increased enemy AAA defense had forced the test to be moved away from the preferred site, Route 912B in Rat Fink Valley. 181/ All sensors except the two SPIKESIDs functioned satisfactorily, and none could be read from EC-121R orbits. 182/

The operational evaluation ran from 22-31 January 1970 and was conducted as a conventional Panther Team operation employing OV-10 FAC and A-1 strike aircraft: 183/

> *The navigator in the OV-10 used a manual "CONFIRM" sheet to record a time history of sensor activations to provide sequences which were then interpreted to indicate the presence, number and approximate location of the trucks.*

During the 10-day period, a total of 31 Portatale-detected sequences indicated truck movement. Fourteen of these were visually investigated by means of the Night Observation Device (NOD, an available-light-augmentation instrument to improve visibility during night operations) carried on participating OV-10s and a 15th sequence was checked by an O-2 FAC. Results were as follows:[184/]

Sensor Activations	402	Trucks Sighted	31
Sensor Sequences	31	Trucks Struck	13
Sequences Investigated	15	Trucks Destroyed	11

In addition, three POL fires and one medium secondary explosion were reported. During the period of the test, Panther Teams had 23 FAC confirmed truck kills, 11 of which were directly attributable to Portatale equipped aircraft.[185/]

The evaluation demonstrated that FAC aircraft with a Portatale capability could effectively read out sensor strings masked from other monitor aircraft and utilize the information to detect, acquire and destroy enemy trucks. The test also determined that normal FAC crew duties and the time required to record and interpret sensors placed a limit on the number of sensors and the extent of the area that could be monitored.[186/]

Another Portatale strike string was emplaced on Route 912B in Rat Fink Valley on 3 February 1970 to be used in conjunction with OV-10 FACs and A-6s with Airborne Moving Target Indicator (AMTI) radar

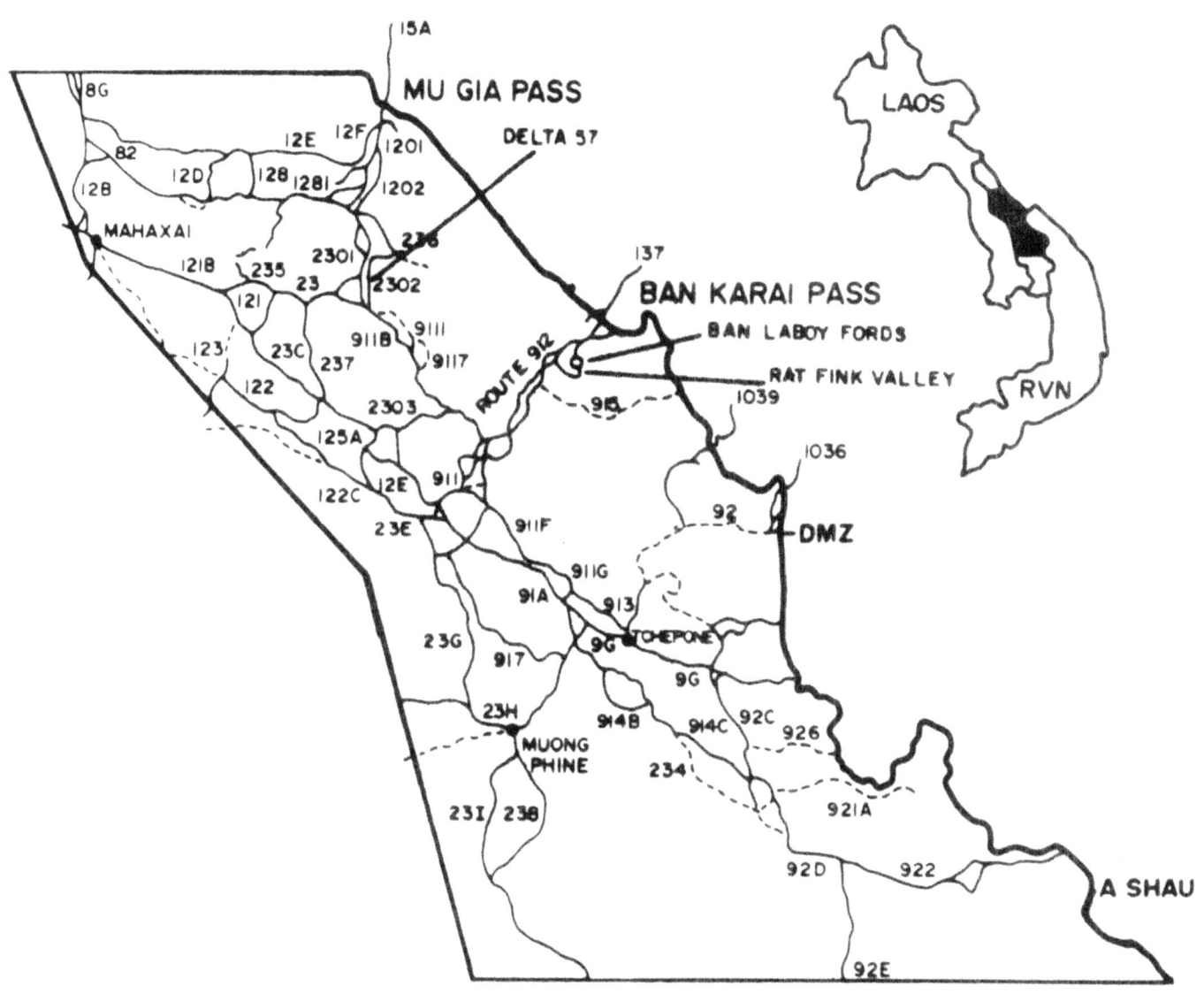

FIGURE 22

capability, but higher priority OV-10 requirements prevented this from being carried out.[187]

Further TFA study of the widespread application of Portatale revealed numerous difficulties if gunships or even substantial numbers of FAC aircraft were to be equipped with the device on a regular basis. A 27 May 1970 study admitted the advantage in providing real time target information, but the cost of the necessary equipment and modifications (estimated at $300,000) for the FAC and gunship fleet, as well as the added burden on aircrews, were seen as serious drawbacks. The navigator's prime duty of keeping the aircraft above the LOC and searching for truck targets with the NOD would prevent him from adequately monitoring the Portatales and keeping the activation log which was necessary for determining the validity of an activation sequence, and, if valid, the direction of travel. For this reason, the Portatale might be little used or ignored completely, thus wasting the resources involved.[188]

TFA also estimated that less than 10 percent of the sensor string location requests were refused because of terrain masking; many of these routes could be monitored just as effectively by putting the string elsewhere on the LOC. The Portatale-equipped FAC aircraft or gunship, because of its low operating altitude, would itself incur terrain masking problems more serious than those affecting EC-121Rs monitoring the sensor field from the normal orbits. Since the Portatale could receive on a small range of channels only, management of a larger

Portatale field would be extremely difficult, and Radio Frequency Interference (RFI) problems would increase. The January 1970 test had avoided this problem by using only two strings. TFA also pointed out that subsequent use of the Portatale had resulted in unspectacular BDA.[189/]

Portatale in CREDIBLE CHASE

The use of Portatale as an airborne sensor read out device surfaced again in September 1971 in connection with the CREDIBLE CHASE program to develop a minigunship based on the Short Take Off and Landing (STOL) Turbo-porter aircraft. During a 14-16 September CREDIBLE CHASE Conference at Eglin Air Force Base, Florida, the use by this aircraft of real time sensor information to assist in the location of targets was discussed. This information was to be provided by on-board read out of sensors through Portatale III devices; the necessary electrical connections were already being installed on all aircraft under existing contracts. In addition, DSPG recommended the installation of RO-376 Event Recorders in CREDIBLE CHASE aircraft to further assist sensor interpretation. At the cut off date for this report, details of this further modification had still to be settled, and no information was available concerning the anticipated employment of airborne Portatale IIIs.[190/]

Radio Frequency Interference (RFI)

IGLOO WHITE sensors have always been considered to be extremely vulnerable to hostile jamming efforts.[191/] Studies in 1966 during the early stages of the sensor program examined IGLOO WHITE's vulnerability to enemy Electronic Countermeasures (ECM), but decided that protective measures would slow program development and procurement. Consequently the risk was accepted and the project went ahead as scheduled. These studies concluded that the probable ECM target in the IGLOO WHITE system would be the sensor-to-aircraft VHF data relay.[192/]

While North Vietnamese forces failed to employ such tactics against IGLOO WHITE, RFI was noted on sensor monitoring channels on several occasions during COMMANDO HUNT V. An incident on 7 October 1970 featured severe sensor data interference lasting 90 minutes on Blue and Purple Orbits. There was no indication of the intentional introduction of non-data signals into the sensor channels, and the 553d Reconnaissance Wing speculated that it may have been a side effect of either friendly or enemy ECM/anti-ECM activities during B-52 missions.[193/] Similar incidents occurred from December 1970 to March 1971, with durations of a few minutes to nearly an hour.[194/] As predicted by the 1966 studies, the sensor to aircraft data relay proved to be highly vulnerable to RFI.

In early March 1971, the Air Force Special Communications Center at Headquarters Air Force Security Service in San Antonio, Texas, investigated 29 such incidents occurring since 25 January. A strong correlation was found was found between the interference and periods of ECM jamming performed by B-52s and their EB-66 escorts. North Vietnamese SPOON REST Surface-to-Air missile (SAM) acquisition radar frequencies operated near the IGLOO WHITE sensor-to-aircraft data relay; the necessity of jamming these radars raised the likelihood that this interference could be expected to recur in the future.[195/] Sensor data loss because of such incidents was small, however, and RFI represented an inconvenience, rather than a major obstacle to the successful operation of IGLOO WHITE.

At a sensor conference at Sandia Laboratories (the firm responsible for developing much of the IGLOO WHITE technology) in Albuquerque, New Mexico, on 28-30 April 1971, 7th AF reported the jamming problems and requested that the vulnerable channels be deleted and replaced by others in another frequency range.[196/] COMUSMACV approved the change on 9 May and the seven most vulnerable sensor data channels were exchanged for seven new ones.[197/]

A September 1971 TFA message stated that there had never been an attempt by the enemy to interfere electronically with IGLOO WHITE operations, but requested that ". . . every precaution be exercised to insure that knowledge of the potential vulnerability of the IGLOO WHITE system to ECM be safeguarded." The success of enemy jamming efforts "would be a function of the approach used," the message continued, but the size of the sensor field, its dispersal, and the foliage found in STEEL TIGER were all expected to limit the success of such an attempt.[198/]

Enemy Attempts to Neutralize IGLOO WHITE Sensors

Interrogation of enemy captives and ralliers disclosed enemy awareness of sensors and countermeasures against them. Enemy personnel moving along infiltration trails in Laos received occasional briefings concerning sensors from North Vietnamese troops manning Commo-Liaison stations situated along their route. A typical briefing covered the appearance of sensors, common locations, correct procedures upon discovering such a device, methods of rendering them ineffective and the danger they represented.

One North Vietnamese rallier reported that sensors were described to his group as being one meter long and 62mm in diameter, and painted in a camouflage pattern (similar to that of uniforms) to resemble tropical trees. Sensors had four antennae, two for detecting voices and two for sending signals to waiting aircraft.[199/] Most sources reported that the sensors were believed dropped by U.S. reconnaissance aircraft, although one prisoner was told that some were hand-implanted on trails by Army of the Republic of Vietnam (ARVN) Special Forces personnel.[200/]

When moving through areas where sensors were suspected, personnel were instructed to walk slowly and quietly and refrain from speaking. Important messages were to be whispered only, and sticks for fires were to be cut, not broken. Any movement which the sensors detected could result in immediate artillery or air strikes.[201/] The ground and trees in bivouac areas were always closely searched for air-dropped sensors and mines.[202/]

Upon discovery of a sensor, infiltrating personnel were instructed to inform cadre or Commo-Liaison station personnel immediately. Sensors were deactivated by burning or stabbing with bayonets,[203/] or were turned upside down and their antennae jammed into the ground. One rallier who reported that he had broken sensors open claimed that the larger devices contained some 54 "tubes and bulbs." This individual drew two sketches, which resembled transistors, for his interrogator.[204]/ None of the sources reported serious morale problems on account of sensors, although one group was said to have been nervous while passing through a suspected area.

The nature of his sensor-deactivation procedures indicates that the enemy was unaware that sensors automatically deactivated when tilted a certain angle from the vertical. The concern over limited individual conversation and movement while travelling through an area with possible sensor activity revealed that enemy forces believed sensors employed primarily acoustic, rather than seismic detection methods. Since all of the sources were infiltrating ground troops not associated with enemy trucking operations in Laos, no comment is possible about the awareness of enemy vehicle units of sensors and their seismic characteristics.

CHAPTER IV

IGLOO WHITE MONITOR AND RELAY AIRCRAFT

An essential component of the IGLOO WHITE system was the availability of a reliable airborne platform from which to read out emplaced sensors or transmit the data to the ISC. The primary relay/read out aircraft for the IGLOO WHITE program had always been former Navy EC-121Rs operated by the 553d Reconnaissance Wing at Korat Royal Thai Air Force Base, Thailand. Commencing operations in November 1967, the 553d RW eventually deployed 24 aircraft (with the call sign BATCAT) which flew 10-hour missions at altitudes of 16,000' to 18,000'. At that altitude sensor transmissions could be received for a radius of 43 nautical miles with about 90 percent accuracy. [205/]

Due to the age of the EC-121R increasing amounts of time were spent on maintenance, and spare parts were difficult to obtain. Other EC-121R shortcomings were its large crew of up to 22 men and limited altitude capabilities. IGLOO WHITE planners also believed that a higher-flying monitor relay platform would be able to cover the Laotian sensor field with fewer orbits and sorties. These considerations and the desire to reduce system costs made the early procurement of a follow-on relay aircraft a matter of great importance to IGLOO WHITE. [206/]

PAVE EAGLE I

Since early 1968, Headquarters Tactical Air Command (TAC) had sought the development of a drone ground sensor monitor which could

Lockheed EC-121R BATCAT
Figure 23.

operate in antiaircraft artillery (AAA) high threat areas where the vulnerable EC-121R and its large crew could not be risked. The aircraft chosen for this task was a Beechcraft Debonair modified with a turbo-super charged engine, additional fuel capacity, sensor data relay equipment and the capability to operate in a drone (or NULLO - No Live Operator Aboard) mode. This aircraft, designated YOU-22A and given the project name of PAVE EAGLE I, was expected to be suitable for orbits of 12 hours duration in a NULLO mode and six hours with a pilot aboard. PAVE EAGLE I was designed to operate solely as an airborne relay platform and even when manned had no capability to manually read out sensors or pass target advisories. 207/

Five OU-22A aircraft were in place at Nakhon Phanom Royal Thai Air Base, Thailand, by 7 December 1968 and began test and evaluation flights as part of the IGLOO WHITE program. 208/ Although these test flights were conducted in the drone mode, a pilot was always aboard to prevent the loss of aircraft since radio frequency interference at NKP reduced the reliability of the drone control equipment. 209/ During the evaluation (in which PAVE EAGLE Is flew one of three sensor monitoring orbits) 210/ certain deficiencies were identified, such as the lack of sufficient power, deicing gear, and cabin pressurization. More serious shortcomings involving in-flight engine failures resulted in the QU-22A being restricted from flights over hostile territory on 1 July 1969. 211/ QU-22A crashes in June and August prompted the return of all remaining aircraft to the United States in December 1969. 212/

PAVE EAGLE II

PAVE EAGLE II (QU-22B) succeeded PAVE EAGLE I. The B model was similar to its predecessor, but was based on the Beech Model 36. Cost considerations precluded the installation of certain desirable features such as cabin pressurization or a turbo-prop engine, although a larger reciprocating engine was installed.[213/] PAVE EAGLE II operated at altitudes of between 20,000' and 23,000' (6,000' higher than the EC-121R) and was normally flown in a remote control mode, although a pilot was on board in case of difficulties.[214/] A fleet of QU-22Bs was expected to perform the EC-121R mission at one-fifth the cost and one-fourth the personnel requirements of the larger aircraft.[215/]

Since the QU-22B was unable to read out sensors on board the aircraft, it was necessary that the location of the monitoring orbit for extreme southern STEEL TIGER be adjusted to permit the relay of data to TFA. EC-121R BATCATs flying Purple Orbit were able to read out sensor strings manually on board the aircraft, and conducted a traffic advisory service (FERRET III) for FACs and gunships in the area by use of X-T Plotters. The great distance of Purple Orbit from NKP, however, prevented relay of data to TFA for the accomplishment of these functions. The greater altitude capabilities of the QU-22B allowed a new orbit to be established (White Orbit) which could monitor all of Purple's sensors and at the same time effectively relay the data to TFA for read out. The optimum location for White Orbit was developed by test flying during late 1970-early 1971. Part of this program was a special STEEL TIGER test orbit designated Lavender.[216/]

Beech QU-22B

(PAVE EAGLE II)

FIGURE 24

The first five QU-22Bs arrived in SEA in early June 1970 to supplement the 18 remaining EC-121Rs.[217] Full coverage of Green Orbit (three sorties/12 hours a day) began on 1 October, and on 15 October QU-22Bs assumed coverage of Blue Orbit (another three sorties/12 hours per day). Rough running engines and the crash of an aircraft in Laos in late December, however, caused the temporary grounding of the entire fleet by the end of the year. By 31 January 1971, the 16 PAVE EAGLE IIs at NKP were again covering Green Orbit and had extended their flights to Blue Orbit (nine sorties/32 flying hours daily). At this time, the QU-22B was fulfilling all of its intended commitments,[218] and the 553d RW's EC-121Rs were covering Purple Orbit.

At no time during their operational evaluation had either PAVE EAGLE I or II flown missions solely in a NULLO mode. Reasoning that no mission degradation would result from operations in a manned mode only, PACAF on 8 March 1971 authorized the removal of drone equipment from all QU-22B aircraft and the disposition of the control vans and radio units. During the first 1500 hours of operation, two in-flight auto-pilot malfunctions would have resulted in loss of the aircraft if a pilot had not been aboard. PACAF concluded that the greater altitude capability of the QU-22B would allow orbits to be adjusted to avoid AAA threats without adversely affecting the quality of sensor read out.[219]

Since early December 1970, the QU-22B program had encountered increasing difficulties with the aircraft's powerplant, fuel system, maintenance and supply. In spite of these problems and the resultant lost orbit time, the increase in the QU-22B's operational commitment had been necessary to allow complete coverage of the two orbits in light of the dwindling EC-121R fleet. These increasing difficulties and the 8 February 1971 crash of a QU-22B in which the pilot was lost finally led to the EC-121R having to replace PAVE EAGLE II on half of Blue Orbit.[220/] On 23 March the QU-22B was relieved of the rest of Blue Orbit and continued on Green Orbit only, at a rate of three sorties a day.[221/]

The 56th Special Operations Wing (SOW) at NKP began a graduated test program on 26 April 1971 to evaluate the QU-22B's reliability and to discover the cause of the engine difficulties which had continually plagued both PAVE EAGLES. The first stage of the program consisted of four QU-22B sorties a day to cover Green Orbit and two other sorties flying a modified Green Orbit in the vicinity of NKP for test and training purposes. The number of sorties gradually increased until by 17 May a total of nine aircraft were flying daily (six on Green Orbit and three conducting local test flying).[222/] During the 26 April-7 June evaluation, 48 incidents of engine roughness were noted, with all but 16 of these occuring in the same four aircraft.[223/]

By 10 July 1971, PAVE EAGLE II was covering Green Orbit with four sorties a day (13 flying hours) and had assumed the late afternoon/early morning portions of Blue Orbit (three sorties/nine hours).[224/] Three QU-22B crashes in August, however, resulted in an 18 August directive from 7th AF that all aircraft were to be removed from IGLOO WHITE/COMPASS FLAG support activities.[225/]

Within a week of the new restrictions, the 56SOW began a 45-day test program consisting of flights under visual conditions within gliding distance of NKP. The tests were intended to determine engine reliability and sought to duplicate operational missions. Aircraft were flown between 16,000' and 20,000' in hopes of assessing the effect of altitude on engine performance. Additionally, a copilot was added to all flights to record instrument readings, identify deficient areas and increase crew confidence.[226/] A CINCPACAF message on 20 August reported that personnel and facilities at NKP were adequate for support of the program and that "additional on-site assistance may be counterproductive." The message admitted that engines were still the major cause of accidents, and that no significant trend or cause was identifiable; similar problems existed ". . . today that did a year ago."[227/]

By 15 September, the QU-22B had improved to such an extent that the aircraft was again allowed to fly Green Orbit and resume COMPASS FLAG testing. This schedule was to continue until the 1 October end of the 45-day test program.[228/] On that date, the QU-22B transferred Green Orbit to the Airborne Command and Control Center C-130E (ABCCC) and devoted all of its available resources to flying the more demanding (both in distance from NKP and hours of sortie time per day) Blue Orbit.[229/]

ABCCC as IGLOO WHITE Relay Aircraft

As early as February 1971, agencies associated with IGLOO WHITE began to investigate alternate relay aircraft in case the QU-22B's difficulties proved unresolvable. On 25 February, TFA reported to 7th AF that the T-39, U-21, U-2, and C-130 had been considered as IGLOO WHITE relay aircraft, but only the C-130 had been successfully flight-tested in this role. The test had been held the previous month at Eglin Air Force Base, Florida. TFA requested that an ABCCC C-130E be sent to NKP for ground tests to determine the compatibility of IGLOO WHITE and ABCCC equipment. [230/]

Ground tests were successful and an ABCCC aircraft with IGLOO WHITE Prime Mission Equipment (PME) borrowed from a QU-22B was test-flown on Green Orbit on 18-20 June. No interference or operational degradation was noted between the two missions, and the C-130E's performance as a sensor monitor was considered identical with that of the PAVE EAGLE system. No additional personnel were required aboard the ABCCC aircraft, and the installation of the IGLOO WHITE PME and antennae could be accomplished during periodic C-130 maintenance. [231/] The ABCCC C-130E functioned solely as a monitor/relay station, and possessed no manual read out or FERRET III capability.

The 18 August decision to remove all PAVE EAGLE IIs from IGLOO WHITE orbits also accelerated the program to install QU-22B relay equipment packages in the ABCCC C-130Es. These modifications were

Lockheed C-130E Airborne Battlefield Command
and Control Center (ABCCC).

FIGURE 25

completed by the end of September. All nine remaining EC-121Rs were
ordered retained in SEA through 1 October as an additional measure
to ensure mission coverage.[232/] The return of the QU-22B to operations
in mid-September and the success of the ABCCC C-130E, however, allowed
plans to go ahead for reducing the EC-121R fleet to six in early
October.[233/]

During late August and much of September 1971, ABCCC C-130Es
regularly monitored the IGLOO WHITE sensor field in northern STEEL
TIGER and relayed the information back to TFA. The sensor field in
extreme southern STEEL TIGER was monitored from White Orbit by the ABCCC
aircraft on a test basis, but during most of the period this area was
covered by Purple Orbit EC-121Rs. When restricted to White Orbit,
ABCCC found its command and control mission degraded, since the C-130E
was unable to adjust its location to enhance communications with strike
aircraft and Laotian ground forces. Similar difficulties occurred on
Blue Orbit. Since ABCCC could best combine both missions on Green
Orbit, it began flying at this location on 1 October when QU-22B
improvements allowed the smaller aircraft to assume responsibility for
Blue Orbit. Southern STEEL TIGER continued to be monitored by EC-121R
BATCAT on Purple Orbit.[234/]

C-130B as IGLOO WHITE/COMPASS FLAG Support Aircraft

In a continuing search for additional alternate airborne platforms for IGLOO WHITE and COMPASS FLAG, a standard C-130B was fitted
with PME for both of these programs and test flown during late September

from NKP.[235] The tests were completely successful and at the time of this report, requests and proposals for acquiring and specially modifying three C-130Bs for these missions were under consideration at 7th AF.[236]

CHAPTER V

DART I AND II AND DUFFLE BAG

Both of the Deployable Automatic Relay Terminal (DART) programs initially were deployed in support of U.S. Army operations in the RVN and were not considered part of IGLOO WHITE. They are included in this paper because they were developed and operated by the U.S. Air Force and employed IGLOO WHITE concepts and technology. DART I was transferred to TFA in July 1971 and integrated into IGLOO WHITE. DART II was terminated in September 1970, but knowledge of its difficulties and shortcomings is important for a proper appreciation of the role of sensors in Southeast Asia.

While IGLOO WHITE was directed almost exclusively against enemy vehicles and vehicle-related activities, the DART/DUFFLE BAG programs were concerned primarily with detecting the presence of enemy personnel. After its transfer to Quang Tri and subsequent move to TFA, however, DART I also played an important role in monitoring enemy vehicle activity on LOCs in northern MR I and the southern DMZ. Frequent use was made of hand-or-helicopter emplaced sensors in all these programs, although IGLOO WHITE-style F-4 sensor delivery became standard practice in both the DARTs.

DART I

DART I originally became operational at Bien Hoa Air Base, RVN, on 1 March 1969 to maintain sensor surveillance of infiltration from

FIGURE 26

Cambodia into the RVN. It was also part of the DUFFLE BAG program of unattended ground sensors employed within Vietnam. The DART read out facility consisted of transportable components including a directional S-Band antenna atop a 60-foot relay tower. DART was designed to read out sensors, interpret the data, and relay near-real time (less than one minute old) information on enemy personnel and vehicular movements to strike agencies in much the same manner as the ISC at NKP. [237/]

The primary sensor used in DART I was the Hand Emplaced Seismic Intrusion Detector (HANDSID I). Magnetic Intrusion Detector (MAGID) or Passive Infrared Intrusion Detector (PIRID) devices could be hand-wired to HANDSID to increase its sensitivity. [238/] Because of the flat terrain in the MR III area of the RVN, sensor data was relayed to the Bien Hoa facility by means of a permanent ground relay atop a 3,235 foot mountain (Nui Ba Den). EC-121R BATCATs flying on Amber Orbit were available to automatically relay this data to Bien Hoa during periods when the ground relay was nonoperational. Both the Bien Hoa and Nui Ba Den facilities were operated by the Air Force, while the Army was responsible for emplacing sensors. Artillery fire responses to sensor activations came from the 25th Infantry, 1st Infantry and 1st Air Cavalry Divisions. [239/]

By early 1970, the Army's Battlefield Area Surveillance System (BASS) was being introduced into the DART I area. Once BASS was in operation, II Field Force Vietnam (IIFFV) felt that a transfer of DART I to another operating area would be agreeable to the three divisions which it served.[240/] BASS employed the same sensors as DART I, and also used ground relay stations to pass the information to a read out facility.

DART I terminated operations at Bien Hoa on 18 March 1970 and began preparations for moving the sensor read out equipment and the 73 Air Force officers and enlisted men to the new operating location at Quang Tri in RVN MR I. The relay equipment situated on Nui Ba Den was also removed, with only the monitor antenna left behind to support the BASS system.[241/] Upon arrival at Quang Tri DART I began monitoring sensor strings located in or near the Demilitarized Zone (DMZ) and in the northwestern portion of the XXIV Corps area, including the A Shau Valley.[242/]

Due to the mountainous and rugged terrain in MR I and the presence of enemy controlled high threat areas which restricted the implant of sensors by hand or helicopter, certain features of the relocated DART I operation differed from those followed in MR III. In addition to HANDSID sensors and the previous emplacement techniques increasing use was made of F-4 delivered ADSID, ACOUSID, and COMMIKE sensors identical to those employed by IGLOO WHITE. While some sections of the DART I field were read out by BASS and hand-carried Portatale units, the primary monitoring was done by an EC-121R BATCAT flying Blue Orbit for 18-24 hours a day. XXIV Corps at Da Nang

determined desired sensor locations based on inputs from field units
and then forwarded the requests to TFA. TFA managed the sensor field
(plotted implant locations, prepared sensor addresses, and resolved
terrain-masking problems) and arranged for F-4 implant sorties. Target
data was relayed from Blue Orbit to the DART I facility at Quang Tri
where it was read out on four 120-pin X-T Plotters (See Figure 27) and
sent directly to an Army Tactical Operations Center (TOC) which determined
the type of response.[243/] Primary Army users were the TOCs of the 1st
Brigade of the 5th Infantry Division at Quang Tri and the 101st Airborne
Division at Camp Eagle.[244/]

The DART I report for 1-31 October 1970 reflected typical activities
of the system after its move to Quang Tri. During this period, the DART
I sensor field established an enemy pattern of movement into and out
of the RVN along Route 9. Based on this analysis an infantry force
was able to establish contact to engage the enemy, killing five North
Vietnamese soldiers and capturing three AK-47 rifles. Other infantry
engagement and Cobra helicopter gunship strikes based on sensor activations resulted in an additional 29 enemy KIA and 36 bunkers destroyed.
The 1st Brigade, 5th Infantry Division and the 101st Airborne Division
recorded 1,048 sensor activations during the month and responded with
238 artillery fire missions which expended 1,296 rounds.[245/]

The DART I sensor field originally consisted of Phase I and II
sensors like its IGLOO WHITE counterpart in Laos. During the 1970-71
campaign (COMMANDO HUNT V) the DART field as well as that in Laos

was converted to Phase III sensors. The DART I field was scheduled to convert fully to Phase III by 15 December, the date that the QU-22B aircraft would begin to monitor half of Blue Orbit.[246/] Since the QU-22B was equipped to monitor and relay data only from Phase III devices, no more Phase I/II sensors were implanted after 1 October. Those remaining were not monitored after 15 December and gradually died out.[247/]

The use of OV-10 aircraft to implant sensors was first mentioned in a November 1970 memorandum from a 7th AF staff officer. He reported that the Marines were using this method and recommended that it be seriously investigated by the Air Force on a selective basis.[248/] A 7th AF feasibility study of the suggestion in early December revealed that Military Assistance Command Vietnam (MACV) also had requested an investigation of this delivery method to support Army sensor implants in MR I and possibly replace F-4 implants. The 7th AF study determined that the AAA threat level in the DMZ, Western Reconnaissance Zone (WRZ) and A Shau Valley still required F-4s and that the Portable Multiple Bomb Rack (PMBR) utilized by Marine OV-10s for sensor implants was not available in Air Force supply channels and would take a year to procure, flight test, and install operationally.[249/] During the Dewey Canyon II phase of Lam Son 719 in early 1971, Marine OV-10s continued sensor implants and emplaced 41 ADSID strings in support of Route 9/Khe Sanh security.[250/]

The area monitored by DART was temporarily expanded during Lam Son 719 to include 19 selected strings in STEEL TIGER.[251/] Information obtained on movers was passed through XXIV Corps Forward Headquarters to ARVN commanders and provided valuable information on enemy truck and personnel movements.252/ TFA was called upon to monitor the DART field during Lam Son 719 from 7-13 and 14-24 March when the DART facility at Quang Tri was down for maintenance. Since the DART field was monitored by the Blue Orbit BATCAT, the activations were transmitted to TFA and read out on the newly installed X-T Plotter. Although TFA possessed the capability of backing up DART for short periods of time without additional manning, four DART personnel were sent TDY to the ISC to provide assistance during the March difficulties. Activations were called directly to Army units from TFA by landline.253/

On 5 July 1971, 7th AF proposals of the previous month to close down the DART I facility and transfer it to TFA were put into effect. Seventh Air Force justified the move for three reasons:254/

    a. The transfer of DART I would be consistent with programs for the future utilization of TFA and would provide a fifth antenna for IGLOO WHITE and COMPASS FLAG.

    b. A combination of the DART and STEEL TIGER sensor read outs during future campaigns would provide real time target correlation and strike capability against enemy infiltration through the DMZ and along the Laos/RVN border.

    c. The anticipated withdrawal of U.S. Army forces from the Quang Tri area in the near future raised concern for the security of the DART facility and personnel.

In preparation for the move TFA began to monitor the DART field on 11 May be means of the ISC computer during normal computer duty hours and by the X-T Plotter at all other times, for a total of 19 hours daily. Upon completion of equipment installations on 1 August, the DART Plotter took over from the TFA Plotter, although the computer still monitored both the DART and IGLOO WHITE sensor fields from 1700-0600 hours daily.[255/]

DART activation sequences (relayed to TFA by Blue Orbit) were called by TFA in near-real time to the 1/5th and the 101st TOCs. From the TOC, mover information was passed to air strike forces (particularly AC-119G Stinger gunships) through the Tactical Air Control Party (TACP) at the TOC or the I Direct Air Support Center (I DASC).[256/] TFA also issued the DART daily intelligence summaries which had formerly originated from Quang Tri.[257/] A total of 18 DART personnel were transferred to TFA to operate the equipment, and the remaining 34 DART manning positions were deleted.[258/]

DART II

DART II was built originally as a backup for DART I or the ISC, or for use as a training facility in the CONUS. With the success of DART I in 1969, DART II was deployed to SEA in September 1969 to assist in antiinfiltration surveillance along the Cambodian border,[259/] with primary areas of interest being the tri-border area and the Plei Trap Valley.[260/] The system became operational at Pleiku on 28 September 1969 in support of I Field Force Vietnam (IFFV). Sensor read outs

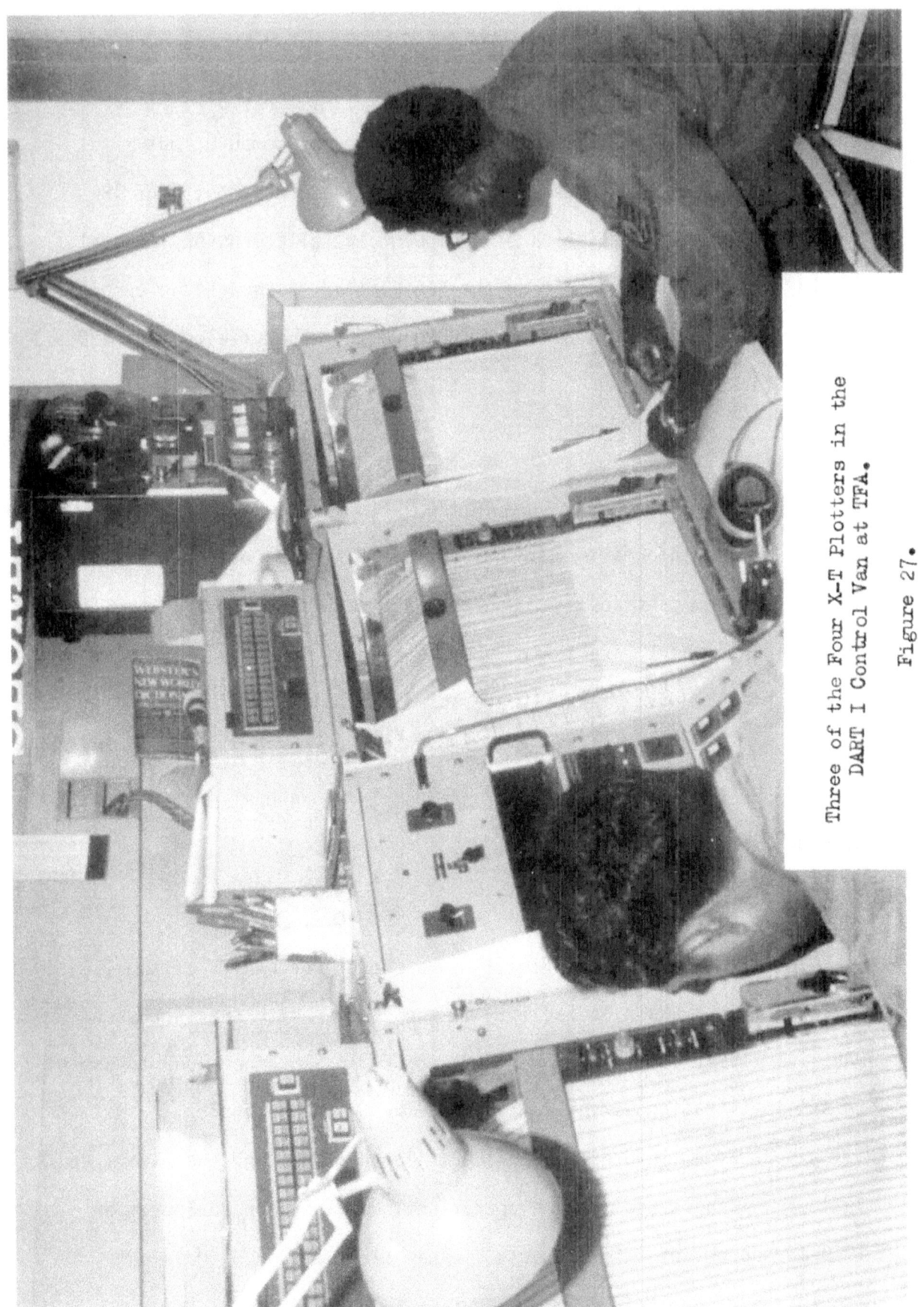

Three of the Four X-T Plotters in the
DART I Control Van at TFA.

Figure 27.

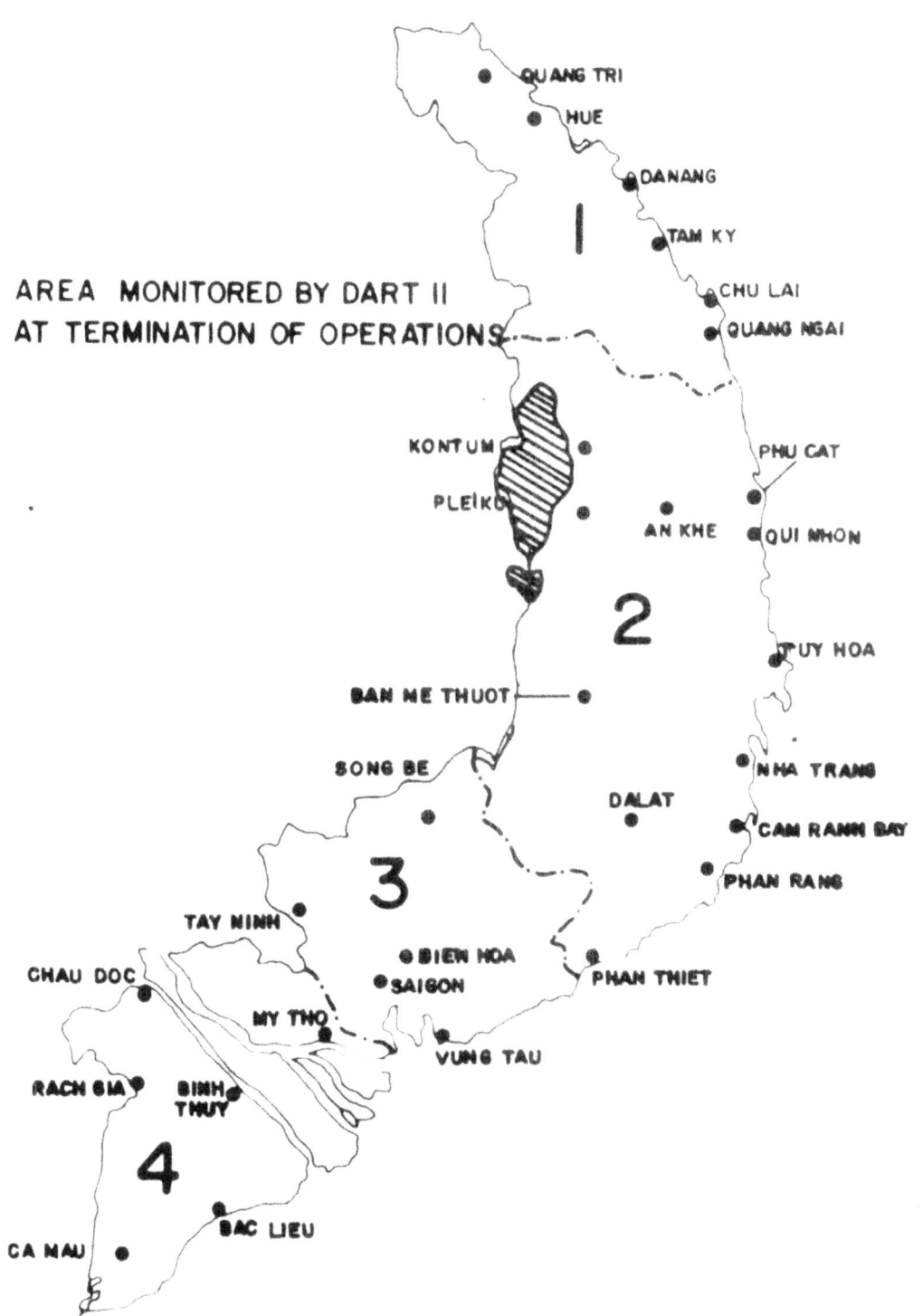

FIGURE 28

were relayed from DART II to the 52d Artillery Group where the type and extent of response were determined.[261/]

DART II differed from DART I in three ways. While DART I did not employ an airborne sensor read out until it moved to Quang Tri, from the beginning DART II utilized EC-121R BATCATs flying Orange Orbit to transmit sensor data to Pleiku. Second, DART II always employed IGLOO WHITE ADSIDs and Phase I/II HELOSIDs and ACOUBUOYs implanted by Army helicopters. Terrain and enemy activity precluded the use of hand-emplaced sensors. Third, 22 Vietnamese Air Force (VNAF) personnel were integrated into the operation in late 1969.[262/]

By early 1970, both 7th AF and IFFV began to express dissatisfaction with DART II and question its effectiveness as a real time targeting system. A 28 March message from the Vice Commander, 7th AF to MACV/J3 (responsible for the DART program) recalled that during January and February there had been an average of six fire support missions a day in support DART II. A 27 February order from the Commanding General, IFFV, however, had directed that artillery fire in support of DART II would be limited only to selected targets, such as those indicating movement. For the previous 30 days, 7th AF complained, there had been only three artillery fire missions against DART II targets. The Army had also recently relocated the 175mm guns covering the DART field in the southern Plei Trap Valley out of range of the sensors. A further shortcoming was that only six air strikes, resulting in one confirmed enemy killed in action (KIA), had been directed against DART II derived targets since the system began operations in September 1969. Seventh Air Force felt that these results and the apparently diminishing Army interest hardly justified the continued commitment to the program of 380 Air Force personnel and six EC-121Rs. [263/]

A second "hard look" was taken at DART II in August. At that time, 7th AF pointed out to MACV/J3 the low number of Army and Air Force strike responses to DART II and the almost total absence of confirmed BDA, as well as the lack of significant intelligence. Other factors cited included: [264/]

    a. The difficulties of maintaining the DART II field in light of the continuing U.S. withdrawal from western MR II.

    b. Eighty-five percent of DART II Air Force personnel were scheduled to rotate at mid-September.

    c. The tri-border sensor field would expire around mid-September and require re-seeding.

    d. The impending introduction of the QU-22B relay aircraft on Orange Orbit would require converting all DART II sensors and facilities to Phase III equipment.

The Commander, U.S. Military Assistance Command, Vietnam (COMUSMACV) and 7th AF also determined that cessation of DART II operations would not significantly affect tactical operations and that DART II did not meet the desired criteria for Vietnamization. [265/] Based on these considerations, DART II was terminated and Orange Orbit cancelled on 29 September 1970, exactly one year after the program originally became operational.[266/]

The DART II end of tour report, dated 12 October 1970, listed a number of factors which had limited the effectiveness of the program:[267/]

    a. Real time target acquisition and effective BDA were limited by the small size of enemy personnel concentrations, his ability to rapidly redeploy and practice concealment, and the large number of trails available for his use.

    b. Repeated reactions by Tac Air and artillery compromised sensor locations, resulting in use of alternate trails by the enemy.

    c. Terrain and the presence of triple canopy jungle limited the availability of collateral intelligence to assist in planning sensor emplacements. Enemy control of the sensor area prevented friendly reconnaissance teams or an agent network from assessing lucrative target areas. Canopy also hindered the accurate placement of sensors in close proximity to specific trails.

    d. The DART II field was limited to an average of 200 sensors because of the need to share channels and addresses with TFA and DUFFLE BAG.

    e. Phase I sensors could not be shut down and continued to broadcast until the end of their 180-day life span. Once strike reactions compromised their locations, enemy forces moved to an alternate area, but the sensor continued to broadcast and prevented the use of that address in a more lucrative area.

    f. The average reaction time of artillery was 20 minutes. Tac Air responded only 11 times and usually involved long delays before a FAC arrived and then more time for strike aircraft to appear. These delays rendered reactions ineffective against an elusive, mobile enemy.

    g. Triple canopy jungle, terrain, and the absence of friendly forces prevented accurate assessment of reaction results.

Table 8 sums up the results of DART II's year of operation.

TABLE 8

DART II RESULTS [268]

28 September 1969 - 29 September 1970

Total Operationally Valid Targets Detected:	4178
Total Artillery Fire Missions:	938
Total Rounds of Artillery Expended:	7469
Total TAC Air Strikes:	11
Total Number of Sensor Strings:	155
Total Number of Sensors Implanted:	607

Damage Inflicted on Communist Forces
by Actions Based on DART II Reports

Killed in Action:	6
Bunkers Destroyed:	2
Secondary Explosions:	2
Sustained Fires:	2
Captured Equipment:	One AK-47 Rifle Two Grenades One Rucksack with Documents

The final paragraph of the DART II Weekly Activity Report for 23-29 September 1970 appropriately marked the close of the program: [269]

> *In keeping with MACV. . .and 7AF. . .DART II ceased operations. So, as the sun slowly sank in the western sky, DART II bid a fond AMF*

(Adios, my friends) as it sadly swung shut its doors to the ghastly background cry of a dying SPIKESID pleading, "Tac Air, Artillery, Car 54- Where are you-u-u-u-u-u-u-u?"

U.S. Air Force Support of DUFFLE BAG

The transfer of DART I to TFA and the cancellation of DART II did not terminate the Air Force's role in the RVN sensor program (designated DUFFLE BAG). MACV priorities for supporting DUFFLE BAG emphasized coverage of the DMZ and areas in the RVN adjacent to the Laos/Cambodian borders. In practice, this placed the majority of the DUFFLE BAG effort in northern RVN within the area controlled by XXIV Corps. [270/]

Seventh Air Force responsibilities in DUFFLE BAG included providing the capability to monitor a maximum of 400 sensors in the DMZ, WRZ, and A Shau Valley for 19 hours a day (this was the DART I program). Activation sequences would be called within one minute of validation to Army TOCs for possible fire response. Seventh Air Force provided F-4 implant sorties adequate to maintain a maximum of 40 sensor strings, with XXIV Corps retaining the option to implant or re-seed any of the 40 strings. Three IGLOO WHITE channels were made available to DUFFLE BAG for relay purposes on aircraft covering Blue or any follow-on orbit, [271/] in addition to the five channels permanently assigned to the program. All eight were read out by TFA. [272/]

Twenty-fourth Corps in turn was responsible for managing sensor addresses on its eight channels and for providing the Air Force with a continuously updated listing of the 40 strings eligible for F-4 implant. Twenty-fourth Corps also provided a liaison officer to TFA on a TDY basis to coordinate sensor management, implant and monitoring requirements.[273]

DUEL BLADE

DUEL BLADE was another term associated with the DUFFLE BAG program. DUEL BLADE originally referred to a Strong-Point Obstacle Subsystem (SPOS) along the northeastern RVN border and had previously carried the name DYE MARKER.[274] By late 1968, the SPOS had evolved into a program in which friendly maneuver forces used mobile tactics with air, artillery, and naval gunfire support to respond to targets detected by ground sensor devices (this was known as DUEL BLADE II). The DUEL BLADE II area included all territory in the RVN south of the Provisional Military Demarcation Line (PMDL) and north of Route 9. By early 1971, the term DUEL BLADE II had been terminated and absorbed into DUFFLE BAG. In its last year, DUEL BLADE II referred more to a geographical area than a program or concept.[275]

BASS

Occasional references have been made in this report to the Army's Battlefield Area Surveillance System (BASS). BASS was different from the DARTs in that it did not consist of a specific, relatively fixed set of components or hardware. Rather, BASS was a concept which covered a variety of different sensors and read out facilities, as well as applications and uses.[276] BASS systems were often local in nature and involved the monitoring of approaches to defended villages and fixed military installations. The system was capable, however, of covering a larger area, as occurred when DART I was replaced by BASS in MR III. Airborne read out of BASS fields or air emplacement of sensors by other than Army organic aviation generally was not practiced, although instances occurred in northern RVN, where Air Force F-4s and Marine OV-10s occasionally delivered sensors in support of Army requirements and read outs were available from Blue Orbit. No major USAF role was anticipated in the development and future use of BASS.

Vietnamization of Sensor Programs (TIGHT JAW)

On 19 March 1969, the U.S. Joint Chiefs of Staff directed that the in-country sensor program be expanded to include Republic of Vietnam Armed Forces (RVNAF) personnel. These efforts to provide the Vietnamese with their own sensor capabilities were known as Project TIGHT JAW. On 15 June 1969, COMUSMACV Operations Plan 103-69 provided for a combined US/RVNAF border surveillance and anti-infiltration program covering selected western border areas of the RVN from the DMZ to the Gulf of Thailand and an expansion of existing sensor missions throughout the RVN. Eventual Vietnamese unilateral operation of this program was envisioned.[277/]

A July 1970 examination of northern MR I revealed the requirement for Vietnamese-operated sensor fields in this area. At this time, MACV proposed eventual Vietnamese Air Force (VNAF) operation of

DART I (Quang Tri) and DART II (Pleiku), each with a 476 sensor capacity. The VNAF would have the ability to implant sensors and monitor them with an airborne platform dedicated solely to sensor read out. Although a particular aircraft was not specified, PAVE EAGLE II was indicated elsewhere.[278/]

PACAF, 7th AF and the USAF Advisory Group agreed that the VNAF should have a capability to implant sensors, but opposed Vietnamizing the DARTs and giving VNAF an additional aircraft to operate. Instead, a simple air relay-monitoring system compatible with BASS was proposed, since personnel resources, and budgetary limitations precluded any VNAF effort approaching even a modest IGLOO WHITE concept. It was also believed likely that any VNAF role in future Vietnamese sensor programs would be that of a support role responsive to ARVN through direction of the RVNAF Joint General Staff (JGS).[279/]

By October 1970, COMUSMACV agreed that Vietnamization of PAVE EAGLE II and the remaining DART was impractical. Instead of a specialized aircraft dedicated solely to airborne sensor read out, emphasis was placed on the development of an unsophisticated Palletized Airborne Relay (PAR) system which would interface with BASS equipment already programmed for the RVNAF.[280/] By September 1971, the USAF was in the process of procuring PAR packages which would initially be fitted in VNAF C-47s and be available for installation in C-7s when these aircraft entered the VNAF inventory in 1973. If necessary PARs could also be in C-119s and C-123s.[281/] Upon introduction of PARs, the VNAF was expected to be fully capable of relaying sensor data to ground stations from C-47s. However, RVNAF JGS would first have to authorize VNAF to utilize aircraft for this purpose in competition with other requirements (such as airlift). The USAF was expected to have no major role in the introduction of the PAR when the time came, and advisors were expected to be drawn from ARVN personnel familiar with sensors.[282/]

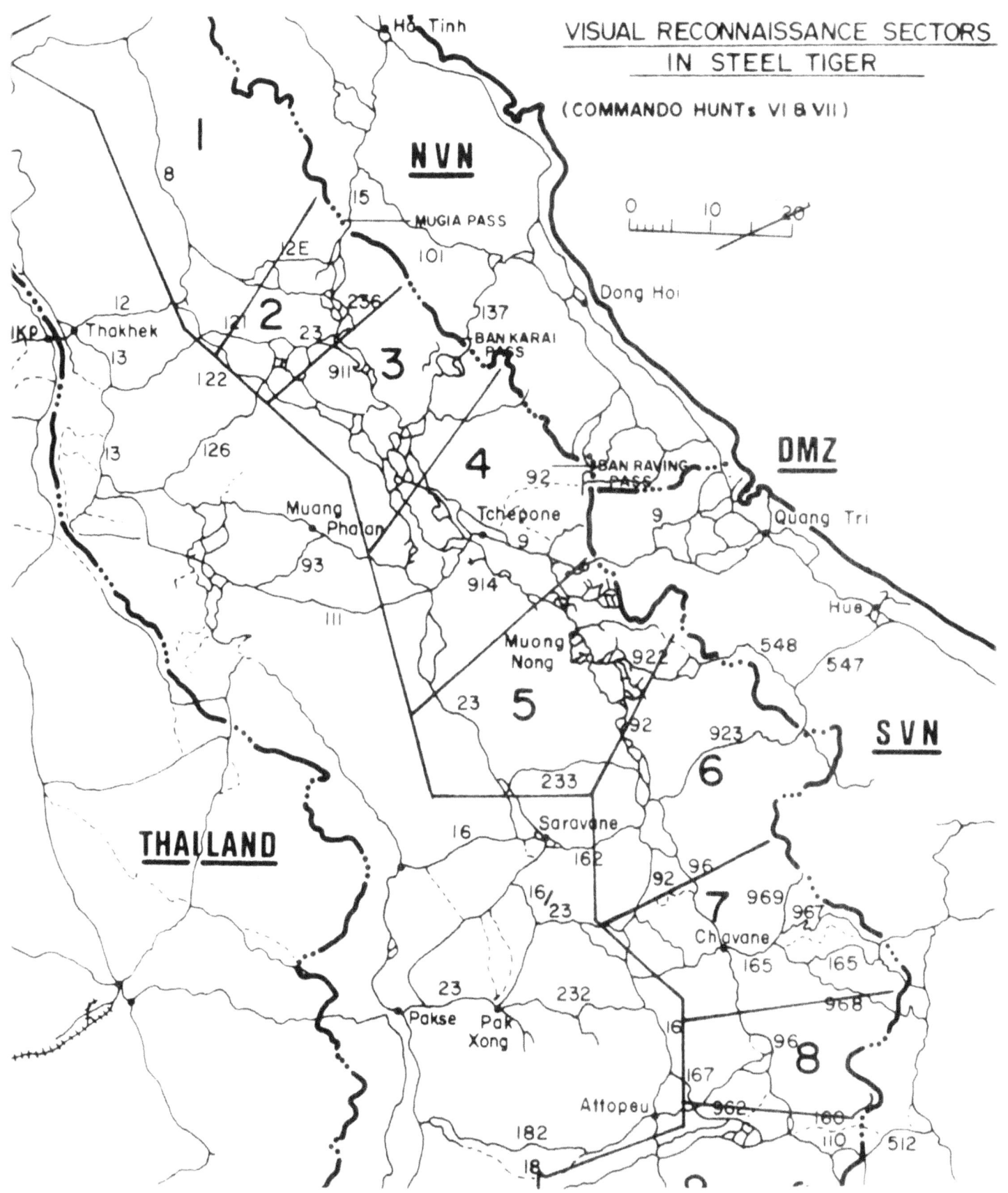

FIGURE 29

CHAPTER VI

THE FUTURE OF IGLOO WHITE: COMMANDO HUNT VII AND BEYOND

Planning for COMMANDO HUNT VII

The COMMANDO HUNT VII campaign was just beginning as this report was going to press. The most significant change planned for IGLOO WHITE for this campaign was TFA's resumption of operational control of strike aircraft operating as part of the STEEL TIGER interdiction program. The actual details of the new procedures were still being developed at the cut off date of this report, but certain features promised to be different from the SYCAMORE Control operation of COMMANDO HUNT I.

Early planning for TFA's new function envisioned the ISC operating as an extension of the 7th AF Combat Operations Center (COC, call sign BLUE CHIP) and utilizing near-real time sensor information to direct strike aircraft (including gunships) to lucrative truck-killing areas. Ideally, the process would be a complete cycle through to damage assessment, with a restrike capability if any lucrative targets remained. 283/

One proposed form of the new procedures under consideration involved the division of the nine VR sectors into three groups (possibly sectors 1-3, 4-5, and 6-9). Aircraft operating over each set of VR sectors would be under the control of a sector operator "station" each of which would include strike control, radio communications and intelligence personnel. Like the COMMANDO BOLT system, strike nominators would closely monitor sensor strings in their assigned area by use of

IBM 2250 and 2260 display consoles. Specific coordinates of developing targets would then be passed by radio to FAC and strike aircraft in the area. In the majority of cases, moving vehicle targets would be acquired by the aircraft either visually or by radar before strike, rather than struck on the basis of predetermined LORAN coordinates. Under this proposal, a Chief Controller would supervise the "stations" and have the authority to divert strike resources from one set of VR sectors to another in which the number of strikeable targets exceeded the aircraft available to send against them.[284/] EC-121R BATCATs most likely would continue on-board sensor read out and FERRET III operations on Purple Orbit (covering sensor strings in the VR sector 6-9 area), since the distance precluded data relay to TFA without expanded communications facilities.

The intelligence section of the "station" would be composed of personnel knowledgeable of the local route structure, enemy activity patterns and the results of recent FAC and photographic reconnaissance of their assigned geographic area, as well as its target/BDA history. Based on developing sensor patterns and utilizing techniques similar to those of the Night Fixed Targeting Program, perishable semifixed targets would be located with varying degrees of precision and passed to the strike nominator for immediate FAC reconnaissance or strike. Working with the "stations" would be weather and communications-maintenance personnel, as well as another intelligence targets team responsible for combining previous target intelligence with inputs from the "stations" to develop fixed-area targets throughout STEEL TIGER.[285/] The use of Special Intelligence (SI) would be an essential part of all target development functions, with much of this material being made available to IGLOO WHITE through the COMPASS FLAG program.

Questions unsettled at the end of this reporting period included the number of "stations" to be established, the final breakdown of VR sector responsibilities, whether all or only some strike aircraft would be assigned to TFA, and the number of hours a day the system would operate. This last question was of considerable importance, since a round-the-clock interdiction operation at TFA based on IGLOO WHITE infomation would require 24-hour a day coverage of the sensor-monitoring orbits with the resultant increased demands on manpower, aircraft, and material in all phases of the program.

Other changes anticipated for COMMANDO HUNT VII included the expansion of the KEYWORD File from its current approximately 24,000 entries to almost 100,000. This was to be accomplished by adding the 7th AF computerized intelligence data base to KEYWORD, and would expand the STEEL TIGER data base as well as introduce information from northern Laos (BARREL ROLL), Cambodia, and the RVN. In addition, the 7th AF AAA file and its BDA listing were also to be added to KEYWORD. Also available for target development purposes (although not a part of KEYWORD) was an SI collection of 10,000 cross-indexed file cards along with specialized supporting material.

Upon successful conclusion of the KEYWORD expansion, TFA would combine a variety of intelligence resources at one location: sensor information; KEYWORD File; access to FACs and their reports; Airborne Radio-Direction Finding (ARDF) capabilities; opportunities to coordinate with Controlled American Source offices; and SI programs (including COMPASS FLAG). In addition, TFA possessed the only Air Force map-making facility in SEA. By assuming operational control of strike aircraft during COMMANDO HUNT VII, TFA hoped to make direct real time use of its concentration of intelligence/targeting resources.[286/]

TFA also anticipated that the COMMANDO HUNT VII IGLOO WHITE sensor field would be larger than any of its predecessors, because of extension to the WRZ of the RVN and certain LOCs in STEEL TIGER west.[287/] Another proposal under consideration was to reduce the maximum number of sensors for certain strings from eight to four or five,[288/] which would allow an increase in the number of sensor strings from the approximately 185 possible with eight sensors per string. The 185 string figure had been made possible by the addition of eight more IGLOO WHITE sensor frequencies during COMMANDO HUNT VI.

Remote Ground Sensor Planning and Programming Objectives (REGSENSPO)

In December 1970, Headquarters USAF issued a document entitled REGSENSPO which sought to provide ". . . guidance for coordinated midrange and long-range U.S. Air Force planning and programming of remote ground sensors and associated resources."[289/] REGSENSPO envisioned the "integration of ground-based surveillance capabilities and the resultant intelligence data into tactical networks for use by air base defense components and the Tactical Air Control System for the attack of ground targets in day, night and all-weather conditions." Tactical Air Command (TAC) was then in the process of coordinating with Air Force Systems Command (AFSC) and the Air Staff to incorporate sensor technology into contingency forces.

United States Air Forces Europe (USAFE) were asked in this document to consider remote ground sensors as a means of providing surveillance of forces hostile to NATO, especially their probable airfield, missile, AAA, and truck park/storage sites. Other factors to be considered by USAFE were the emplacing and airborne monitoring of sensors in hostile air environments and their use in a stay-behind role by retreating friendly forces.

PACAF's tasking letter which accompanied the basic REGSENSPO document to its subordinate numbered Air Forces (5th AF, 7th AF, 13th AF, and 7/13th AF) requested comments concerning organizational relationships of future sensor operations. For example, at what level of assignment could sensor resources be most effectively utilized; should they be aligned with the intelligence or the command/control function; and should all components (emplacement vehicles, read out equipment, required facilities) be centrally controlled?[290/]

The 7th AF reply to PACAF (dated 16 January 1970) concerned the SEA area during the 1974-78 timeframe when it was assumed that all U.S. forces supporting IGLOO WHITE would have been withdrawn. The most useful sensor types were seen as ADSIDs, ACOUSIDs, and possibly EDETs (this was before the EDET test of March-June 1971). To establish a minimal 40-string field for six months (with a 60-day average life per sensor), approximately 1600 sensors would have to be on hand or procurable on a short-term basis. A steady supply of new sensors would be necessary if either the 40 string or the six-month figure were exceeded. Sensor implant missions would almost certainly have to be performed by LORAN-equipped F-4D aircraft, although OV-10s possibly could be used for visual delivery in AAA low-threat areas. 291/

The use of an airborne read out of sensors was seen as providing maximum felxibility for sensor field location and configuration, although 7th AF felt that there were no systems available at that time (March 1971) which could adequately perform this task. Even FERRET III operations with the X-T Plotter were viewed as ". . . only marginally adequate for even the less demanding applications." 292/ For relaying sensor activations to a ground read out terminal, 7th AF discussed both the QU-22B and a Palletized Airborne Relay (PAR) which was being developed for installation aboard various VNAF cargo aircraft. PAR was seen as offering maximum flexibility at the least cost for a contingency sensor system, and was recommended as the best choice for monitoring any future fields.

Further, 7th AF suggested that the ground terminal facility for interpreting sensor activations probably would be similar to DART I or the more sophisticated Sensor Reporting Post (SRP, this was an air-transportable, mobile ISC which featured a small digital computer and could monitor a field of 400 sensors. It was under development at Eglin AFB, Florida).[293] This terminal would necessarily be readily deployable to SEA and reasonably mobile once it had arrived in theater. Given the geography of SEA and the PACAF area of operations, 7th AF suggested that the potential of a shipboard SRP-type facility should be investigated as a means of providing maximum deployment flexibility.[294]

Finally, 7th AF answered PACAF's questions on who should control a sensor system, and to what degree it should be centralized. Management and control of the system should be within the operations rather than the intelligence function, 7th AF stated, although a close operations-intelligence relationship was necessary to its successful operation. In addition, central management of all system components was seen as necessary to insure proper coordination of sensor logistics, field location and configuration, sensor implant, airborne relay schedules, and ground terminal operations. The 7th AF reply concluded with a comment on the resource competition between a sensor system and strike forces:[295]

> *The competitive priority of a contingency sensor system should be low compared to the priority of strike forces in a reduced budget environment. However, a minimal system could be maintained with little impact on strike force capability, considering the relative costs of a minimal sensor system versus the costs of strike aircraft, associated equipment and facilities.*

PACAF's 15 March 1971 response to the original Headquarters USAF REGSENSPO document repeated many of 7th AF's ideas. The primary use of ground sensor technology to the Air Force in the future was seen by PACAF to be target development on a real time basis, with intelligence collecting being secondary. This technology could be best exploited in PACAF's opinion, by integrating the capabilities of the SRP or similar facility in a manual mode with the Combat Reporting Center (CRC) and then including both functions in the Tactical Air Control System (TACS).[296/]

Like 7th AF, PACAF recommended the use of ADSID/ACOUSID sensors against vehicles, but stressed the need for an antipersonnel capability as well. F-4 sensor implants also were seen as necessary, and airborne data relay requirements could be best satisfied by use of the PAR. Deployment mobility was regarded as vital for the ground read out facility, which would utilize either a DART type facility or the SRP. The PACAF letter also mentioned the use of sensors to augment existing Air Control and Warning (AC&W) systems by providing a capability for detecting low-flying aircraft. This capability would be most useful in Korea, but should also be deployable throughout the Pacific area. PACAF also drew attention to the vulnerability of sensors to hostile ECM, and stressed that efforts should continue to develop protection against this threat in future applications.[297]

In an article appearing in the June 1971 issue of The Air Force Magazine, Major General William J. Evans, former Deputy to the Director of the DCPG/DSPG, discussed areas in which sensor research and development were continuing. Development of longer-life batteries was a prime item of interest, as were sensors which would properly implant and operate in terrain in cold-climate parts of the world. Sensor cases were desired which would blend with different types of topography and vegetation. The General also mentioned the need for new types of detectors with better target discrimination (a possible reference to EDET III), and sensor frequency bands suitable for worldwide use. Also required were sensor transmitters less vulnerable to jamming, as well as an airborne monitor/relay platform able to operate in hostile air environments. Finally, Major General Evans expressed hopes that the accuracy of sensor implants could be improved by different sensor configurations and the development of more precise navigation systems for delivery aircraft. Sensors placed closer to the roads which they monitored would require less detection range and lower battery power, thus resulting in smaller, lighter, and cheaper sensors.[298]

MYSTIC MISSION

On 4 March 1971, the DSPG assigned the name MYSTIC MISSION to a project to develop a Phase III sensor system for use in Europe. On

9 August, DSPG activated Detachment 1 of Joint Task Force 728 to test and evaluate the new sensor program. To control the CONUS phase of the evaluation, Detachment 1 became operational on 13 September 1971 at Field 2, Eglin Air Force Base, Florida. This was a joint services project, with a U.S. Army commander, an Air Force vice commander, and a Marine Corps chief of staff. 299/

Conclusion

In October 1971, IGLOO WHITE stood at a crossroads. For the past four years, various sensor applications and uses had been proposed and tested operationally in SEA under combat conditions. For the COMMANDO HUNT VII campaign, the most successful of these programs apparently were to be combined with the authority to control directly a substantial portion of the Air Force's interdiction resources in STEEL TIGER. Although a number of separate and distinct agencies and operations were necessary to the success of the new system, the real time target detection capability of IGLOO WHITE was to be the center of the 1971-72 interdiction effort. Since both 7th AF and PACAF saw the ability of IGLOO WHITE to detect lucrative targets, direct strike aircraft against them on a real time basis, and restrike if necessary , to be the principal justification for such systems in the Air Force inventory, the results of COMMANDO HUNT VII promised to have a decisive impact on the future role of remote ground sensor technology in the U.S. Air Force.

APPENDIX I

Instructions for use of CONFIRM sheet readouts on pages 109 and 110.

SECTION 1 - Sensor String Number. The first two digits (01-09) identified in which the Visual Reconnaissance (VR) sectors of STEEL TIGER the string was located. There were nine VR sectors for the 1971-72 campaign. The notation at the extreme left identified the Ground Surveillance Monitor (GSM) responsible for monitoring the particular set of strings.

SECTION 2 - Distance Between Sensors. This figure was read from top to bottom in tenths of a kilometer. Thus, 0.26 would equal 260 meters. In certain cases the distance was given between the adjoining strings along the same LOC. For example, the last sensor in string 08-220 and the first in string 08-221 were 140 meters apart along the same road. The figures at the far left represented the year and the Julian (Zulu) date.

SECTION 3 - Individual Sensors in String. Sensor strings normally had a maximum of eight sensors, with additional strings being implanted if more sensors were desired. Since only currently active sensors were listed on the CONFIRM sheets, gaps frequently appeared in the enumeration. The sensors were always numbered from north to south, with the highest number being the southernmost sensor in the string. Strings with only one active sensor were not normally monitored.

SECTION 4 - Listing of Activations by Minute. The CONFIRM sheet displayed 40 minutes of Zulu time, with the most recent period being at the bottom of the sheet.

   a. Since seismic sensors could activate for six 10-second periods each minute, the total number of those periods for which the sensor was activated was displayed in this section. This was updated at the end of each minute when all activations for that period had been received by the computer. Thus, the higher the number (up to six), the more activity was occurring within range of the sensor. Hyper-active sensors displayed continual activations and were regarded as unreliable.

105

b. The sample sheets illustrate patterns displayed by various activation sources. Vehicular traffic generally displayed a diagonal "step" pattern, starting with the first sensor in the string. Southbound vehicles would begin with low numbered sensors, while northbound trucks would first activate the higher numbered ones. Aircraft, ordnance and localized activity displayed distinctive patterns which a trained operator could easily distinguish from trucks.

c. Acoustic sensors were "polled" (commanded to transmit audio) when a nearby seismic or ignition sensor revealed activity. The resulting audio assessment by the Radio Operator helped determine the nature of the activation. In addition, COMMIKEs were polled at random throughout the night for any indication of enemy activity. In either case, the Radio Operator upon detecting positive signals entered his assessment of the sounds into the computer (and hence onto the GSM's IBM 2250 CONFIRM display) according to the following letter code:

AB	Tracked vehicles and motorcycles	M	Motion
AC	Motorcycles and aircraft	MO	Motion and ordnance
AF	Trucks and motorcycles	MP	Motion and aircraft
AK	Tracked vehicles and aircraft	MS	Motion and small arms
AT	Trucks and aircraft	O	Ordnance
AV	Tracked vehicles and trucks	OP	Ordnance and aircraft
AZ	Trucks closest to sensor	OS	Ordnance and small arms
B	Background noise	PA	Prop aircraft
CA	Motorcycles	SP	Small arms and aircraft
CM	Motorcycles and motion	TA	Trucks
CO	Motorcycles and ordnance	TM	Trucks and motion
CS	Motorcycles and small arms	TO	Trucks and ordnance
CV	Motorcycles and voices	TS	Trucks and small arms
G	Small arms	TV	Trucks and voices
HA	Helicopter	U	Unassessable
JA	Jet Aircraft	V	Voices
KA	Tracked vehicles	VM	Voices and motion
KM	Tracked vehicles and motion	VO	Voices and ordnance
KO	Tracked vehicles and ordnance	VP	Voices and aircraft
KS	Tracked vehicles and small arms	VS	Voices and small arms
KV	Tracked vehicles and voices	W	Weather

SECTION 5 - **Mode.** Indicates whether the sensor is being read out in a real time (R) basis with activations being passes as they occur, or non-real time (N), in which information is stored by the sensor for transmission at a later time upon command.

SECTION 6 - **Type of Sensor.** Sensors were identified by means of the following letter codes:

W - ADSID (Seismic only)
N - ACOUSID (Seismic and acoustic)
E - EDET (Ignition only)
Y - COMMIKE (Acoustic only)
Q - COMMIKE/EDET (Acoustic and ignition)

SECTION 7 - **Sensitivity.** Refers to sensor detection range and strength of activations. The sensitivity of sensors can be adjusted to eliminate extraneous stimuli which could cause false activations. This also allows adjustments to be made to individual sensors in a string in relation to their distance from the LOC which they are monitoring, so that a uniform pattern is presented on the CONFIRM display.

SECTION 8 - **Bit Rate.** Refers to the rate at which sensor-transmitted data is received by the computer. This is usually at 300 pieces of information (or "bits") per minute, although it can be reduced to 75. The lower rate is used to reduce the effect of various forms of radio. Frequency Interference (RFI).

SECTION 9 - **Reliability.** Sensors were rated according to the following code:

1. Unknown reliability. Given to all newly-implanted sensors.

2. A 2, 3 or 4-rated sensor which has had no activations for three days.

3. Audio sensors. COMMIKEs or ACOUSIDS which have lost their seismic capability but still retain audio.

4. Sensors that activate for weather, aircraft or random activations only. Does not participate in truck sequences.

5. Hyperactive sensors. Activates for long periods of time for apparent reason.

6. A sensor previously rated 7, 8 or 9 but which has had no activations for a minimum of three days.

7. A useful but not reliable sensor. Activates for less than 40 percent of truck sequences, or gives unusual activations during sequences. Occasionally helps 8 or 9-rates sensors call sequences.

8. Activates for 40-95 percent of truck sequences.

9. Activates for more than 95 percent of truck sequences.

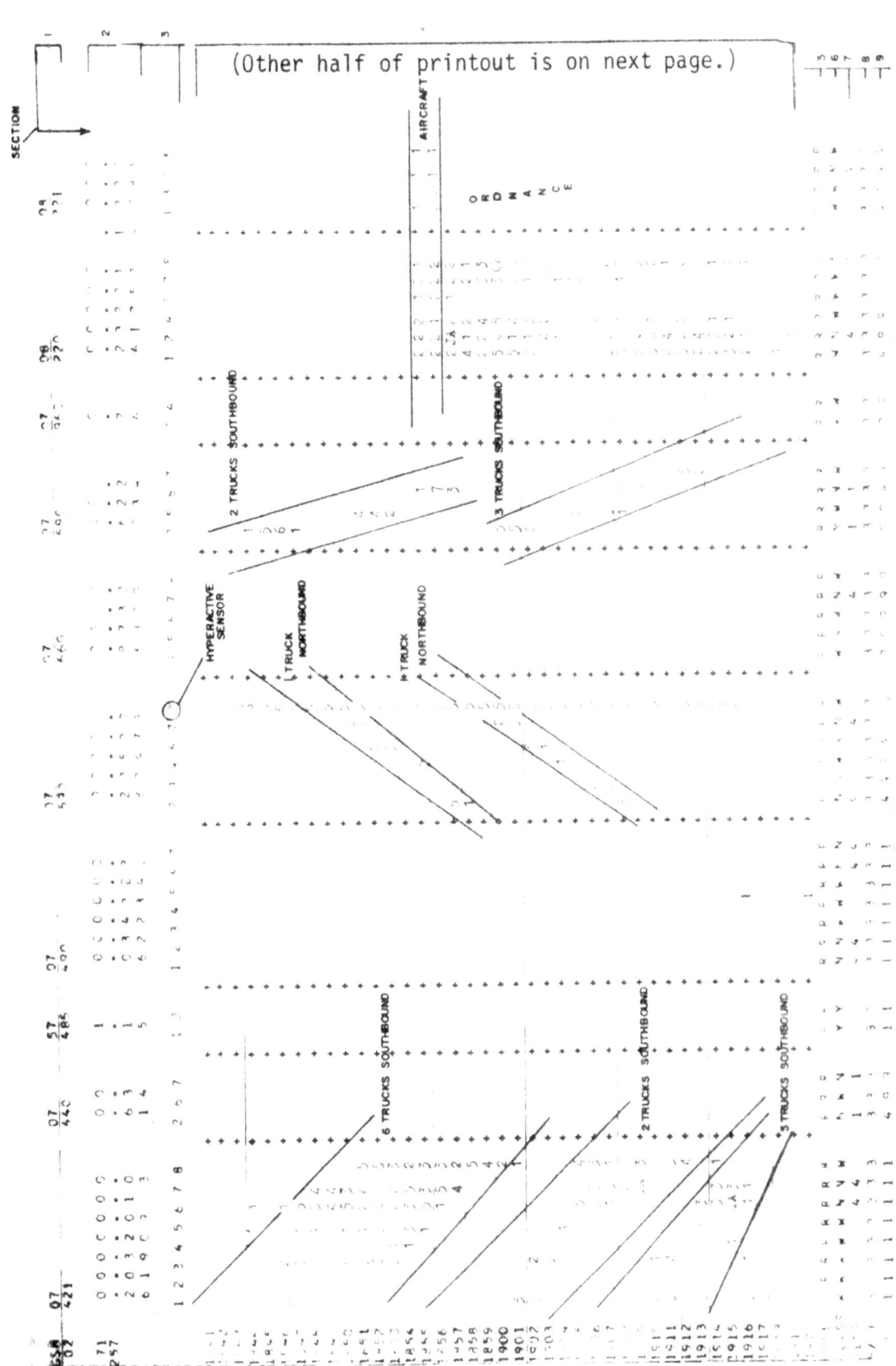

IGLOO WHITE COINCIDENCE FILTERING INTELLIGENCE REPORTING MEDIUM (CONFIRM) Sheet
With Typical Sensor Activation Patterns
(Numbers along right side are keyed to the explanatory text in Appendix I)

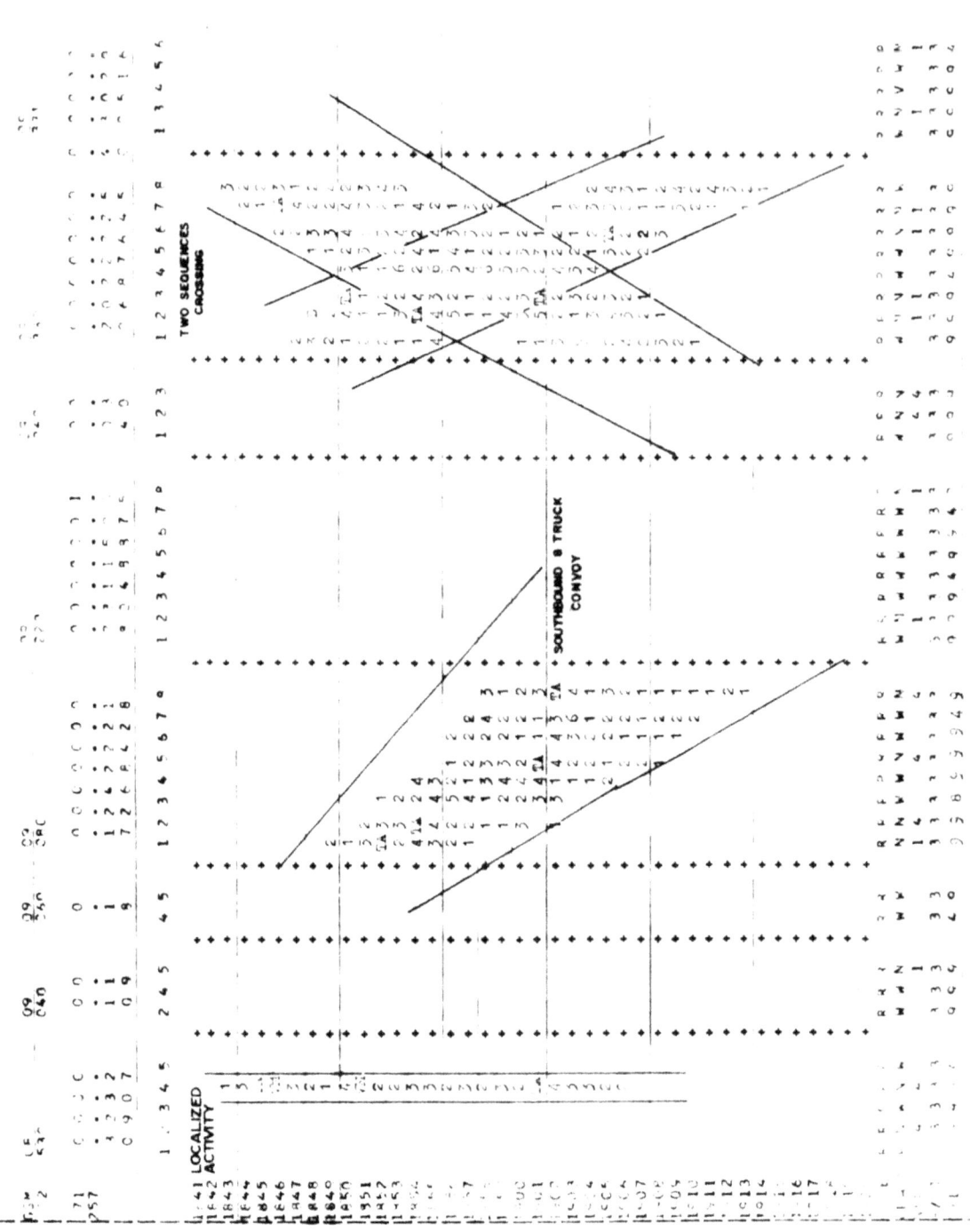

IGLOO WHITE COINCIDENCE FILTERING INTELLIGENCE REPORTING MEDIUM (CONFIRM) Sheet With Typical Sensor Activation Patterns

APPENDIX II

This list of aircraft orbits associated with IGLOO WHITE includes all those mentioned in this report.

ORBIT	AIRCRAFT	PROGRAM SUPPORTED	NO. OF HOURS DAILY	DATE FLOWN OR SEPTEMBER 1971 STATUS
Amber	EC-121R	DART I at Pleiku (Backup)	As required	May 1969 - March 1970
Black (TACC-A)	EC-121R	Cambodian strings (Use of Cambodian ABCCC to monitor sensors)	18	December 1970 - February 1971 (as sensor monitor)
Blue	EC-121R QU-22B C-130 (ABCCC)	DART I, IGLOO WHITE	18-24	Flown daily
Green	EC-121R QU-22B C-130 (ABCCC)	IGLOO WHITE	21	Flown daily
Lavender	EC-121R QU-22B	A test orbit flown to determine feasibility of White Orbit		Late 1970 - early 1971
Orange	EC-121R QU-22B	DART II	10 (Night)	September 1969 - September 1970
Pink	EC-121R	Sensors in NVN	Unknown	3-26 November 1968
Purple	EC-121R	IGLOO WHITE. Distance precluded relay of data to TFA	10 (Night)	Flown when C-130B not available for White Orbit

Red	C-130 (ABCCC)	Test orbit flown to assess quality of data read out from ABCCC C-130 compared with Blue Orbit		July 1971
Rose	EC-121R	Sensors along Route 7 in BARREL ROLL	10.0	August 1969 - January 1970
White	C-130B	Monitors Purple Orbit, but positioned so that higher altitude allows relay of data to TFA for read out	10.5	Flown daily
Yellow	QU-22B C-130	COMPASS FLAG (flies a track rather than an orbit)	10-12	Test stage

AIRCRAFT ORBITS ASSOCIATED WITH IGLOO WHITE

APPENDIX III

SEQUENCES PASSED, SEQUENCES NOT PASSED, AND BDA FOR HEADSHED NIGHT TRAFFIC ADVISORY SERVICE
24 October 1970 - 31 August 1971 (Based on OPREP-4 Data) 300/

	OCT	NOV	DEC	JAN	FEB	MAR	APR	MAY	JUN	JUL
Sequences processed	15	3501	9103	15,721	17,732	18,841	17,988	13,034	3804	1137
Movers processed	22	6190	13,781	26,913	31,471	34,337	26,892	18,483	4966	1436
Sequences passed	4	1652	2836	5690	4793	5221	5843	4441	1506	508
Sequences not passed	11	1849	6267	10,031	12,939	13,620	12,154	8593	2298	629
No aircraft available	7	1154	3157	3530	4249	5607	3562	4745	1600	339
Unable to contact aircraft	0	162	758	1586	1632	1436	1588	1123	170	78
Aircraft working strike or busy	0	373	2025	3891	5412	5052	6441	2208	377	139
Communications difficulties made information untimely	0	7	45	63	203	54	48	41	4	7
Weather precluded use of advisory	0	68	229	946	191	971	249	384	139	62
Below filter level	1	45	5	15	0	0	0	0	0	0
Other	3	39	48	0	0	500	257	92	8	3

Trucks destroyed	0	0	17	350	426	873	1012	134	15	11
Trucks damaged	0	0	4	76	105	233	165	142	32	15
Secondary Explosions	0	0	26	375	275	795	479	160	168	93
Secondary Fires	0	0	23	267	277	494	348	108	74	79
Sequences passed to:										
COMMANDO BOLT	2	729	1014	2299	2658	1996	814	301	99	20
MOONBEAM	0	286	293	721	471	714	1148	823	417	131
FACs	2	313	709	1157	672	707	1400	1474	516	135
Gunships	0	135	502	948	733	1165	2037	1517	346	182
BLUE CHIP (7AF COC)	0	0	3	10	0	0	0	0	0	1
Armed Recce	0	189	315	555	259	639	444	326	128	40

FOOTNOTES

CHAPTER I

1. (S) CHECO Report IGLOO WHITE, July 1968 - December 1969, Hq PACAF, 10 January 1970, p. 1 (Hereafter cited as CHECO IGLOO WHITE II).

2. (TS) CHECO Report IGLOO WHITE, (Initial Phase), Hq PACAF, 31 July 1968, p. 1 (Hereafter cited as CHECO IGLOO WHITE I).

3. (S) Ibid, p. 3

4. (S) Ibid, p. 5

5. (S) Ibid, p. 6

6. (S) Ibid

7. (S) Ibid, pp. 30-31

8. (S) Ibid, p. 10

9. (S) Briefing, subject: "TFA Command Briefing," presented to Colonel D. L. Flowers, Director of Command and Control, Hq 7AF, 18 September 1971 at TFA, NKP RTAB, Thailand. (Hereafter cited as TFA Briefing.)

10. (C) Message, TFA to 7DCOP, subject: Phase III Sensor Frequencies, 200220Z June 1971.

    (S) Interview, topic: IGLOO WHITE. With Lieutenant Colonel Gean G. Kowalski, Chief, Surveillance Systems Branch, Tactical Air Control/Surveillance Division, Directorate of Command and Control, DCS/Operations, Hq 7AF, by Captain Henry S. Shields, Project CHECO at Tan Son Nhut AB, RVN, 12 October 1971. (Hereafter cited as Kowalski Interview.)

11. (S) Kowalski Interview.

12. (S) TFA Briefing

13. (S) Ibid, and conversation with Colonel R. Rumney, former Director of Technical Operations, TFA, at Tan Son Nhut AB, RVN, 14 December 1971

14. (S) Report (Staff Summary Sheet), subject: EDET Sensor Test, 23 June 1971, by 7DOCPS.

CHAPTER II

15. (S)   CHECO IGLOO WHITE II, pp. 5-6

16. (S)   Report, subject: Commando Hunt, 20 May 1971, by 7AF, p. 215 (Hereafter cited as Commando Hunt I)

17. (S)   Ibid, pp. 28-29

18. (S)   Ibid, p. 29

19. (S)   Ibid, p. 214

20. (S)   Ibid, p. 239

21. (S)   Ibid, p. 214

22. (S)   Ibid, p. 43

23. (S)   Ibid, p. 215

24. (S)   Ibid, p. 214

25. (S)   Ibid, p. 43

26. (S)   Ibid, p. 234

27. (S)   Ibid, pp. 43-44

28. (S)   Ibid, p. 68

29. (S)   Ibid, p. 161

30. (S)   Ibid, p. 71

31. (S)   Ibid, p. xix

32. (S)   CHECO IGLOO WHITE II, pp. 12-13

33. (S)   Report, subject: "History of TFA, 1 January - 30 June 1970," 10 July 1970, by TFA, p. 4. (Hereafter cited as TFA History, 1 Jan-30 June 70.)

34. (S)   CHECO IGLOO WHITE II, p. 13

35. (S)   Report, subject: "History of TFA, 1 January-31 March 1971," 10 April 1971, by TFA.

36. (S)   Interview, topic: KEYWORD File. With Captain Susan L. LaFontaine, Targets Analysis Officer, TFA, by Captain Henry S. Shields, 17 September 1971.

37. (S) CHECO IGLOO WHITE II, p. 15

38. (S) TFA History, 1 January-30 June 1970, p. 4.

39. (S) Report, subject: COMMANDO HUNT III, May 1970, by 7AF, p. 167 (Hereafter cited as COMMANDO HUNT III.)

40. (S) CHECO IGLOO WHITE II, p. 11

41. (S) Ibid, p. 17

42. (S) COMMANDO HUNT III, pp. 168-169

43. (S) Ibid, p. 169

44. (S) Ibid, pp. 172-174

45. (S) Ibid, p. 173

46. (S) Ibid, p. 171; pp. 174-176

47. (S) Ibid, p. 174

48. (S) Ibid, p. 176

49. (S) Ibid, p. 175

50. (S) Ibid

51. (S) Ibid, p. 176

52. (S) Ibid, p. 171; pp. 174-176

53. (S) Ibid, p. 177

54. (S) Ibid.

55. (S) Ibid, p. 178

56. (S) Interviews, topic: COLOSSYS and the Role of Computers in IGLOO WHITE. With TFA personnel, including Captain Ray E. Ruprecht, Duty Director, Directorate of Engineering TFA, and Captain Clifford C. Chastain, Chief, Infiltration Surveillance Division, TFA, by Captain Henry S. Shields, at TFA, NKP RTAB, Thailand, 12-19 September 1971. Also personal observations by the author.

57. (S) Msg, 553RW Korat RTAB, Thailand to 7DOT, Tan Son Nhut AB, RVN, subject: FERRET III Operations, 120955Z Mar 70 (CHECO Microfilm S435, FR 214.)

58. (S)   COMMANDO HUNT III, p. 158.

59. (C)   Report (Staff Summary Sheet), subject: "X-T Plotter Sensor Read Out in EC-121R," 11 December 1970, by 7DOPTS (CHECO Microfilm S437, FR 188).

60. (S)   COMMANDO HUNT III, p. 158

61. (S)   Briefing Notes, subject: FERRET III Operations, 18 February 1970 (Hereafter cited as FERRET III Briefing). (CHECO Microfilm S435, FR 213)

62. (S/NF) Memo for Record, "Methods of Providing Target Information to FACs and Gunships," by TFA/TOA, 27 May 1970, Appendix I: Evaluation of Spotlight and FERRET III. (CHECO Microfilm S420, FRs 175-176)

63. (S/NF) Ibid

64. (S/NF) Ibid

65. (S)   FERRET III Briefing

66. (S)   Interview, topic: DART, X-T Plotter, FERRET III. With Captain Clifford C. Chastain, Chief, Infiltration Surveillance Division, TFA, by Captain Henry S. Shields, at TFA, NKP RTAFB, Thailand, 15 September 1971.

67. (S)   Report, subject: "Ban Raving Operations," part of TFA COMMANDO HUNT III Input to 7AF DOAC, 6 April 1970 (CHECO Microfilm S341, FR 193); TFA History, 6 April - 30 June 1970, pp. 49050; Memo to General Buckner, "Commando Bolt, 15 April - 15 June 1970," from 7AF Tactics and Combat Systems Directorate, 16 August 1970 (CHECO Microfilms S346, FR 47)

68. (S)   TFA History, 1 January-30 June 1970, p. 7

69. (S)   Report, subject: COMMANDO HUNT V, May 1971, by Hq 7AF p. 210 (Hereafter cited as COMMANDO HUNT V)

70. (S)   TFA History, 1 January-30 June 1970, p. 13

71. (S/NF) Msg, TFA to 7DO, subject: Expanded COMMANDO BOLT Operations, 141010Z August 1970 (CHECO Microfilms S436, FR 47)

72. (S)   Interview, topic: COMMANDO BOLT Operations. With Major Eric J. Brister, Staff Operations Officer, TFA, by Captain Henry S. Shields, at TFA, NKP RTAFB, Thailand, 14 September 1971, and conversations, same subject, with Colonel Ben A. Barone, Director of Operations, TFA, 18 September 1971

73. (S) COMMANDO HUNT V, p. 206

74. (S) Ibid.

75. (S) Ibid, p. 212

76. (S) Ibid, p. 213

77. (S) Msg, 7DOC to TFA, subject: COMMANDO BOLT Operating Areas, 060200Z March 1971

78. (S) Brister Interview

79. (S) Ibid

80. (S/NF) Msg, TFA to CTF 77, subject: COMMANDO BOLT Liaison Sitrep 20, 120700Z December 1970 (CHECO Microfilm S436, FR 29)

81. (S) Msg, TFA to CSAF/X00G, subject: Request for Sensor Information, 021010Z August 1971

82. (S) COMMANDO HUNT III, p. 160

83. (S) Ltr, TFA/INAA to TFA/IN, subject: Band Concept, Commando Hunt V. 20 March 1971 (Hereafter cited as TFA 20 Mar 71 letter)

84. (S) COMMANDO HUNT V, p. 210-211

85. (S) Report, subject: "History of TFA, 1 October-31 December 1970," by TFA, p. 22

86. (S) COMMANDO HUNT V, p. 211

87. (S) Ibid, p. 205

88. (S) Ibid.

89. (S) TFA, 20 March 1971 letter, p. 1

90. (S) Ibid, Attachment 1

91. (S) Report, subject: "History of TFA, 1 January-31 March 1971," 10 April 1971, by TFA. (Hereafter cited as TFA History, 1 January-31 March 1971)

92. (S)   Interview, topic: "Night Fixed Targeting Program." With
            Captain Susan L. LaFontaine, Targets Analysis Officer,
            TFA, and conversations with Major Barry W. Hubbard,
            Chief, Targets Branch, TFA, by Captain Henery S. Shields,
            at TFA, NKP RTAB, Thailand, 17-18 September 1971

93. (S)   Data obtained from TFA/INT files by Captain LaFontaine

94. (S)   CHECO IGLOO WHITE, p. 29

    (C)   Report (Staff Summary Sheet), subject: "X-T Plotter Sensor
            Read Out in EC-121R," 11 December 1970, by 7DOPTS.

95. (C)   Report (Staff Summary Sheet), subject: "X-T Plotter Sensor
            Read Out in EC-121R," 11 December 1970, by 7DOPTS

96. (S)   COMMANDO HUNT V, p. 210

97. (S)   Report (Staff Summary Sheet), subject: "Sensor Support
            Lam Son 719 and 720," 29 April 1971, by 7DOCPS (Hereafter
            cited as 29 April 1971/DOCPS Report)

98. (S)   Message, Commanding General XXIV Corps to COMUSMACV, subject:
            Lam Son 719 After Action Report, 260722Z April 1971
            (Hereafter cited as 260722Z April 1971/XXIV Corps message).

99. (S)   29 April 1971/DOCPS Report

100. (S)   260722Z April 1971/XXIV Corps message

101. (S)   Ibid.

102. (S)   29 April 1971/DOCPS Report

103. (S)   260722Z April 1971/XXIV Corps message

104. (S)   TFA 20 March 1971 letter, p. 2

105. (S)   TFA History, 1 January - 31 March 1971

106. (S)   Ibid

107. (C)   Message, TFA to 7DOCP, Daily Sensor Activity Report, 030940Z
            October 1971

108. (S/NF) Message, Commander, 7AF to CINCPACAF, subject: Transfer of
            DART, 140005Z June 1971

109. (S/NF) Ibid

110. (C)   Message, TFA to 7DOCP, subject: Phase III Sensor Frequencies, 200220Z June 1971; Msg, Director MAT MGT, Kelly AFB, Texas to 7DOCP, subject: IGLOO WHITE Phase III Sensor Frequencies, 132100Z July 1971

111. (C)   200220Z June 1971 message

112. (S)   Message, CINCPACAF to CSAF, subject: PACAF PAD 71-18, COMPASS FLAG, 262015Z April 1971

113. (S)   Message, 7DOCP to 56SOW, NKP RTAB, Thailand, subject: COMPASS FLAG Orbit Tracks, 032130Z August 1971

114. (S)   Message, CINCPACAF to AFLC, subject: IGLOO WHITE/COMPASS FLAG 091905Z September 1971

115. (S)   Message, 6908SS, NKP RTAB, Thailand, to 13AF, Clark AB, PI, subject: IGLOO WHITE/COMPASS FLAG, 130730Z September 1971

116. (C)   Letter, Commander TFA to all TFA personnel, subject: Shift to Night Shift Operations, 22 June 1971. Interview, topic: DART X-T Plotter, FERRET III. With Captain Clifford C. Chastain, Chief, Infiltration Surveillance Division, TFA, by Captain Henry S. Shields at TFA, NKP RTAB, Thailand, 15 September 1971.

117. (C)   22 June 1971 TFA Commanders letter.

118. (S/NF) Message, 7DIT to TFA, subject: Sensor String Placement Planning for Northeastern Cambodia, 191131Z May 1970 (CHECO Microfilm, S436, FR 97)

119. (S/NF) Ibid

120. (S)   Memorandum for General Hardin (Vice Commander, 7th AF) from Colonel James H. Raddin, Director, Tactics and Combat Systems 7AF, subject: MACV Sensor Surveillance Guidance, 5 June 1970, (CHECO Microfilm S435, FR 139)

121. (S)   Ibid

122. (S/NF) Briefing notes, subject: Cambodian Sensor Plan, 24 June 1970, (CHECO Microfilm S436, FR 98)

123. (S)   Secret Working Paper, subject: Cambodian Sensor Field Plan and Impact on Sensor Requirements, 30 July 1970 (CHECO Microfilm S436, FR 98)

124. (S/NF) Message, 7DO to TFA, subject: Cambodian Sensor Implants, 271005Z September 1970 (CHECO Microfilm S435, FR 141)

125. (S/NF)　Ibid

　　　(S/NF)　Report (Staff Summary Sheet) subject: "Use of FERRET III in Cambodia," by 7DOPTS, 12 October 1970 (CHECO Microfilm S435, FR 184)

126. (S)　　Report (Command Correspondence Staff Summary Sheet), subject: "Analysis: Cambodian Sensor Field Evaluation," by 7DOPTS, 2 November 1970 (CHECO Microfilm S435, FR 140)

127. (S/NF)　Report (Staff Summary Sheet), subject: "Use of FERRET III in Cambodia," by 7DOPTS, 12 October 1970. (CHECO Microfilm S435, FR 184)

128. (S/NF)　Message, 6INT to TFA, subject: Cambodian Sensor Field Plan, 301039Z October 1970 (CHECO Microfilm S435, FR 141)

129. (S)　　Message, 7DOP to 388TFW, 553RW, Info: COMUSMACV, CINCPACAF, 7/13AF, Udorn RTAB, Thailand, TFA, subject: Sensor Monitor on EC-121R TACC-A Mission, 190350Z December 1970 (CHECO Microfilm S435, FR 140)

130. (S)　　Message, 7DOCP to 388TFW, subject: Sensor Monitoring on EC-121R TACC-A Mission, 070830Z February 1971

131. (S/NF)　Report (Staff Summary Sheet), subject: "Cambodian Sensors Monitored by TACC-A," by 7DOCPS, 10 February 1971

132. (S)　　CHECO IGLOO WHITE II, pp. 14-15

133. (S)　　COMMANDO HUNT III, p. 159

134. (S)　　Report (Staff Summary Sheet), subject: "Special BARREL ROLL/ IGLOO WHITE Orbit," by 7DOCPS, 12 August 1971

135. (C)　　Message TFA to PACAF and 7DOCP, subject: Radiation Contract F64620-71-C-0003, 140745Z August 1971

136. (S/NF)　Letter, 7IN to 7DO, subject: Sensor Placement in NVN, 7 December 1970 (CHECO Microfilm S435, FR 166)

137. (S/NF)　Message, COMUSMACV to 7AF, info: TFA, subject: Sensor Placement in NVN, 130800Z December 1970 (CHECO Microfilm S435, FR 129)

138. (S)Q　Message, TFA/INAA to 7DOP and 7IN, subect: Sensor Placement in NVN, 160830Z December 1970 (CHECO Microfilm S435, FR 166)

CHAPTER III

139. (S)   CHECO IGLOO WHITE II, p. 22

140. (S)   Ibid, pp. 22-23

141. (S)   COMMANDO HUNT III, p. 159

142. (S)   COMMANDO HUNT V, p. 205

143. (S)   CHECO IGLOO WHITE II, p. 24

144. (S)   COMMANDO HUNT V, p. 205

145. (C)   Message, CSAF to CINCPACAF, AFSC and TAC, subject: SEAsia Evaluation of EDET Sensor, 101657Z March 1971

146. (C)   Report (Staff Summary Sheet), subject: "EDET Sensor Test," 23 June 1971, by 7DOCPS

   (S)   Hq PACAF DOOCS Review, subject: Project CHECO Report, subject: "IGLOO WHITE, Jan 70 - Sep 71," 10 Jan 72 (Hereafter cited as Hq PACAF DOOCS Review.)

147. (C)   Ibid

148. (C)   Message, TFA to 7DOCP, subject: Production Requirements for EDET Sensor, 131040Z May 1971

   (S)   Hq PACAF DOOCS Review

149. (C)   Message, DSPG to DSPG LNO Saigon, subject: EDET Use for Motorized Sampan Detection, 272220Z August 1971

150. (C)   Message, TFA to 7DOCP, subject: Production Requirements for EDET Sensor, 131040Z May 1971

   (S)   Hq PACAF DOOCS Review

151. (C)   Message, CINCPACAF to TFA, subject: Procurement of EDET III Sensors, 141932Z August 1971

152. (C)   Message, DSPG LNO Saigon to DSPG Washington, subject: EDET Use for Motorized Sampan Detection, 150835Z August 1971

153. (C)   Message, DSPG to DSPB LNO Saigon, subject: EDET Use for Motorized Sampan Detection, 272220Z August 1971

154. (S)   Interview, topic: EDET III Sensors as Used along Waterways. With Captain Richard Herman, Jr., Intelligence Analyst, TFA, by Captain Henery S. Shields, at TFA, NKP RTAB, Thailand, 13 September 1971

155. (C)   Message, TFA to Hq ESD L G Hanscom Field, Mass, subject: EDET Development Concepts, 091034Z June 1971

156. (C)   Ibid

157. (S)   Letter Commander TFA to 7DO, subject: Improved Sensor Requirement, undated-

158. (S)   Ibid

159. (S)   Message, CSAG to AFSC, Andrews AFB, Maryland, subject: EDP Changes, 292053Z July 1971

160. (C)   Message Hq ESD, L G Hanscom Field, Mass, subject: CAEDET, 181512Z August 1971

161. (C)   Message Hq ESD, L G Hanscom Field, Mass to Det 6, ASD, Tan Son Nhut AB, RVN, subject: EDET III and IV, 012141Z July 1971

162. (S)   Report (Staff Summary Sheet), subject: "Status Report, Radar Beacon Transponder (RABET II)," 4 July 1970, by 7DOPTS (CHECO Microfilm S436, FR 196)

163. (S)   Report, subject: "RAVET III History," 4 November 1970 (CHECO Microfilm S436, FR 193)

164. (S)   Message, DCPG to CSAF, subject: Radar Beacon Transponder - RABET, 241902Z December 1970 (CHECO Microfilm S436, FR 193)

165. (S)   Memorandum for Record, "Reasons for Limited Use of ACOUBUOY Sensors in STEEL TIGER in COMMANDO HUNT III, by Lieutenant Colonel James R. Lillethum, Chief of Analysis Division, TFA, 30 June 1970 (CHECO Microfilm S341, FR 204)

166. (S)   COMMANDO HUNT I, p. xv

167. (S)   Lillethum 30 June 1970 Memorandum

168. (S)   Ibid

169. (S)   TFA History, 15 January-31 March 1971, 10 April 1971

170. (C)   Report (Staff Summary Sheet), subject: "New Concept - Acoustic Targeting Area," 18 July 1971 by 7DOCPS

171. (S)   Interview, topic: Acoustic Targeting. With Captain Harry C. Harrison, OIC, Targets Operations Section, TFA, by Captain Henry S. Shields, at TFA, NKP RTAB, Thailand, 14 September 1971. (Hereafter cited as Harrison Interview)

172. (S)   Report (Staff Summary Sheet), subject: "Present Status of Acoustic Targeting Areas (ATA) Program," 28 July 1971, by 7DOCPS.

173. (S)   Harrison Interview

174. (S)   Report (Staff Summary Sheet), subject: "Use of Sensors for BDA," 23 April 1971, by 7DOCPS.

175. (S)   Interview, topic: "Use of Sensors for BDA." With Lieutenant Colonel Theodore E. Hurt, Chief, Air Operations Division, TFA, by Captain Henry S. Shields, at TFA, NKP RTAB, Thailand, 15 September 1971

176. (S/NF) Message, TFA to III MAF/G2 Da Nang, subject: OV-10 Modification, 050940Z January 1970 (CHECO Microfilm S437, FR 201)

177. (S)   Talking Paper, subject: "OV-10 Portatale in COMMANDO BOLT," approximately January 1970 (CHECO Microfilm S437, FR 200)

178. (U)   Message, DIR MAT MGT Kelly AFB, Texas to CINCPAC and 7AF/DMMA, subject: Class IB MODE Request - OV-10A Aircraft, 311853Z December 1969 (CHECO Microfilm S437, FR 201)

179. (S)   Memo for Record, "Status of OV-10/Portatale Modifications," by Major Ronald C. Cadieux, 7DO, 23 January 1970 (CHECO Microfilm S437, FR 201)

180. (S)   Report, subject: "Portatale Evaluation," Appendix F to TFA Input to COMMANDO HUNT III Report, 16 April 1970 (CHECO Microfilm S341, FR 195)

181. (S)   Ibid

182. (S)   Ibid

183. (S)   Ibid

184. (S)   Ibid

185. (S)   Ibid

186. (S)   Ibid

187. (S) Ibid

188. (S) Ibid

189. (S) Memo for Records, "Methods of Providing Target Information to FACs and Gunships," by TFA/TOA, 27 May 1970 (CHECO Microfilm S420, FR 1 5).

190. (S) Message, TAC to CSAF, subject: CREDIBLE CHASE, 261620Z September 1971

191. (S) Report (Command Correspondence Staff Summary Sheet), subject "IGLOO WHITE Phase III Vulnerability to ECM," 20 October 1970, by 7DOPTS (CHECO Microfilm S436, FR 94).

192. (S) Memo for Record, "Comments on ECM vs IGLOO WHITE," by Colonel Joseph H. Wack, Assistant for Electronic Warfare, 23 September 1970 (CHECO Microfilm S436, FR 94)

193. (S) Message, 553RW Korat RTAB, Thailand to 7DOPT, subject: Data Channel Interference, 190831Z October 1970 (CHECO Microfilm S436, FR 101)

194. (S) Memo for Record, "TFA Sensor Data Link Jamming," from 7DOPT to 7INTSM, 8 March 1971

195. (S) 8 March 1971 Memo; Message AGSC San Antonio, Texas to TFA and 7DOPRE, subject: Sensor Degradation, 102212Z March 1971

196. (S) Memo for Record, "Common Module Conference at Sandia Laboratories, Albuquerque, New Mexico, 28 April 1971," in 7DOCPS files.

197. (S) Message, DIR MAT MGT Kelly AFB, Texas, to CSAF/XOOO, subject: IGLOO WHITE Transmitter Channels, 041941Z May 1971; Message 7AF to COMUSMACV, subject: IGLOO WHITE Transmitter Channels, 060700Z May 1971; Message COMUSMACV to 7AF, subject: IGLOO WHITE Transmitter Channels, 090456Z May 1971, all in 7DOCPS files.

198. (S/NF) Message, TFA to 7DOCP, subject: Sensor Countermeasures, 060645Z September 1971, in 7DOCPS files.

199. (C) Interrogation Report #1516-0146-71, subject: "Sensors Briefing to an Infiltration Group," 11 March 1971, by 1021st USAF Fld Activity Squadron

200. (C) Interrogation Report #1516-0289-71, subject: "NVA Briefing on Sensors," 14 May 1971, by 1021st USAF Fld Activity Sq.

201. (C) Interrogation Report #1516-0138-71, subject: "NVA Briefing on Sensors in Laos," 9 March 1971, by 1021st USAF Fld Activity Sq.

202. (C) Interrogation Report #1516-0226-71, subject: "NVA Reaction to Sensoring Devices," 4 May 1971, by 1021st USAF Fld Activity Sq.

203. (C) Interrogation Report #1516-0289-71

204. (C) Interrogation Report #1516-0226-71

CHAPTER IV

205. (S) CHECO IGLOO WHITE II, p. 27

206. (S) Ibid, pp. 29-30

207. (S) Ibid, p. 30

208. (S) QU-22B Chronology, August 1971, in 7DOCPS file. (Hereafter cited as QU-22B Chronology)

209. (S) CHECO IGLOO WHITE II, p. 31

    (S) Hq PACAF DOOCS Review

210. (S) COMMANDO HUNT I, p. 237

211. (S) CHECO IGLOO WHITE II, p. 31

212. (S) QU-22B Chronology

213. (S) CHECO IGLOO WHITE II, p. 31

214. (S) COMMANDO HUNT V, p. 208

    (S) Hq PACAF DOCCS Review

215. (S/NF) Report (Command Correspondence Staff Summary Sheet), subject: "IGLOO WHITE Forces," 28 January 1970, by Lieutenant Colonel Arthur C. Lehrman, Chief, Systems and Resources Branch, 7AF (CHECO Microfilm S436, FR 233)

216. (S) Interview, topic: IGLOO WHITE Orbits and Use of Sensors. With Captain Ray E. Ruprecht, Duty Director, Directorate of Engineering, TFA, by Captain Henry S. Shields at TFA, NKP RTAB, Thailand, 13 September 1971.

217. (S)   QU-22B Chronology

    (S)   Report (Command Correspondence Staff Summary Sheet), subject: "553 Recon Wing C-121G Aircraft," 1 May 1970, by Lieutenant Colonel Edwin J Hatzenbuehler, Jr., Surveillance Division, 7AF.

218. (S)   QU-22B Chronology

    (S)   COMMANDO HUNT V, p. 208

219. (S)   Message, CINCPACAF to AFSC, subject: Deletion of PAVE EAGLE II Drone Capability, 082316Z March 1971.

220. (S)   QU-22B Chronology

    (S)   COMMANDO HUNT V, p. 210

221. (S)   COMMANDO HUNT V, p. 210

222. (S)   Message, 56SOW to 7DO, subject: QU-22B Operations, 220700Z April 1971

223. (S)   Report (Staff Summary Sheet), subject: "IGLOO WHITE Orbits," 7 June 1971, by 7DOCPS.

224. (S)   QU-22B Chronology

225. (S)   Message 7DOC to 56SOW, subject: "IGLOO WHITE Orbits," 180850Z August 1971

226. (S)   Message CINCPACAF to CSAF, subject: "QU-22B," 202135Z August 1971

227. (S)   Ibid

228. (S)   Message CINCPACAF to CINCPAC, subject: "IGLOO WHITE Orbit Requirements," 180135Z September 1971

229. (S)   Kowalski Interview

230. (S)   Message TFA to 7DOCP, subject: "Relay Aircraft," 250255Z February 1971

231. (S)   Report, subject: "CROC-C-130/ABCCC/IGLOO WHITE," in 7DOCPS files

    (S)   Report (Staff Summary Sheet), subject: "ABCCC/ADR, 12 August 1971, by 7DOCPS

232. (S)   Message Commander 7AF to CINCPACAF, subject: "QU-22B Get Well Program," 18 August 1971 (No DTG)

233. (S)   Kowalski Interview

234. (S)   <u>Ibid</u>

235. (S)   Message 13AF to CINCPACAF, subject: "IGLOO WHITE/COMPASS FLAG," 090820Z September 1971

    (S)   Message CINCPACAF to AFLC, subject: "IGLOO WHITE/COMPASS FLAG," 091905Z September 1971

236. (S)   Kowalski Interview

CHAPTER V

237. (S)   CHECO IGLOO WHITE II, p. 44

238. (S)   <u>Ibid</u>, p. 46

239. (S)   <u>Ibid</u>, p. 45

240. (S)   Report (Command Correspondence Staff Summary Sheet), subject: "DART Status," 6 January 1970, by 7DPTS (CHECO Microfilm S437, FR 55)

241. (S)   Report (Command Correspondence Staff Summary Sheet), subject: "Termination of DART I Operations in III CTZ," 12 March 1970, by 7DOTS (CHECO Microfilm S437, FR 42).

242. (C)   Letter, 553RW (DCOOT) to 7DOT, subject: "Conference on 6-8 July to Discuss Standardized Reporting Procedures by the 553RW and DART I to Army Commanders in I Corps," 17 July 1970 (CHECO Microfilm S437, FR 72)

243. (S)   Fact Sheet, "Sensors in SEA, Army, DUFFLE BAG (South Vietnam Only)," 27 October 1970 (CHECO Microfilm TS98, FR 019)

244. (C)   Report (Command Correspondence Staff Summary Sheet), subject: "DART I (Deployable Automatic Relay Terminal)," 21 November 1970, by 7DOPTS (CHECO Microfilm S437, FR 55).

245. (S)   Report, subject: "DART Statistical Report of Sensor Activations, 1-31 October 1970," by Det 2, 505 TAC Control Group (CHECO Microfilm S437, FR 60)

246. (C) Report (Command Correspondence Staff Summary Sheet), subject: "DART I (Deployable Automatic Relay Terminal)," 21 November 1970 by 7DOPTS (CHECO Microfilm S437, FR 55).

247. (C) Message 7DOP to CINCPAC, subject: "Disposition, Phase I/II Assessment Van, DART I," 241045Z December 1970 (CHECO Microfilm S437, FR 51).

248. (S) Memo for Record, "Trip Report for DART I Operations," by Major Alvin L. Pavik, 7DOPTS, 13 November 1970 (CHECO Microfilm S437, FR 56).

249. (S) Report (Command Correspondence Staff Summary Sheet), subject: "Sensor Implant by Air Force OV-10 Aircraft," 3 December 1970 by 7DOPTS (Major Pavik) (CHECO Microfilm S437, FR 164).

250. (S) Message Commanding General XXIV Corps to COMUSMACV, subject: "Lam Son 719 After Action Report," 260722Z April 1971.

251. (C) Report (Staff Summary Sheet), subject: "Status DART I," 22 March 1971 by 7DOCPC.

252. (S) Report (Staff Summary Sheet), subject: "Sensor Support for Lam Son 719 and 720," 29 April 1971 by 7DOCPS.

253. (C) 22 March 1971 Staff Summary Sheet

254. (S/NF) Message Commander 7AF to CINCPACAF, subject: "Transfer of DART," 140005Z June 1971.

255. (S) Message 7DO to TFA, subject: "DART Transfer," 060430Z July 1971

256. (S) Report (Staff Summary Sheet), subject: "DART Reporting," 7 July 1971 by 7DOCPS

257. (S) Message 7DO to TFA, subject: "DART Transfer," 060430Z July 1971

258. (S/NF) Message 7DO to COMUSMACV (J3), subject: "Transfer of DART I Function to TFA," 111000Z May 1971

259. (S) CHECO IGLOO WHITE II, p. 47

260. (S) DART II End of Tour Report, 12 October 1970 (CHECO Microfilm S437, FRs 84-86).

261. (S)   CHECO IGLOO WHITE II, p. 47

262. (S)   Ibid, p. 48

263. (S)   Message Vice Commander 7AF to MACV (J3), no subject, 28 March 1970 (No DTG), (CHECO Microfilm S437, FR 29)

264. (S)   Letter, 7DO to COMUSMACV (J3) (Major General Cowles), subject: DART II, 20 August 1970 (CHECO Microfilm S437, FR 81).

265. (C)   Message CINCPACAF to 7AF, subject: "DART II Redeployment," 090350Z October 1970 (CHECO Microfilm S437, FR 79).

266. (C)   Message 7DO to CINCPACAF, subject: "DART II," 011130Z October 1970 (CHECO Microfilm S437, FR 80).

267. (S)   DART II End of Tour Report, 12 October 1970 (CHECO Microfilm S437, FR 84-86)

268. (S)   Ibid

269. (C)   Message, Det 1 505 TAC Control Group, Pleiku AB, RVN, to 7DO, subject: "DART II Weekly Activity Report 23-29 September 1970," 020130Z October 1970 (CHECO Microfilm S437, FR 82).

270. (C)   Memo for Record, "Notes on IGLOO WHITE/DUFFLE BAG Sensor Program," by Lieutenant Colonel Gean G. Kowalski, 7DOCPS, 3 August 1971, in 7DOCPS files.

271. (C)   Ibid.

272. (S)   Kowalski Interview

273. (C)   3 August 1971 Memo

274. (S)   CHECO Report SEA Glossary 1961-1970, Hq PACAF, 1 January 1970, p. 59

275. (S)   Fact Sheets, subject: "Reporting of MACV Liaison Officer to Paris Peace Talks," by MACV J3-04, 2 February 1971.

276. (S)   Interview, topic: DUFFLE BAG Program and USAF Participation. With Major Robert E. Davis, Communications Systems Officer, Special Operations Branch, Surface Operations Division, ACS/Operations, MACV, by Captain Henry S. Shields at Hq MACV Saigon, RVN, 6 September 1971 (Hereafter cited as Davis Interview).

277. (S)   Report, subject: "Minutes, DUFFLE BAG/TIGHT JAW Conference, 16-17 April 1970," 5 June 1970 by MACV J3-04 (CHECO Microfilm S437, FR 212).

278. (S)   Talking Paper, subject: "VNAF Role in RVNAF Sensor Program," 12 July 1970 by 7DOT (CHECO Microfilm S437, FR 106).

279. (S)   Ibid

280. (S)   Message, COMUSMACV to CINCPAC, subject: "RVNAF I&M Sensor Program," 010244Z October 1970 (CHECO Microfilm S437, FR 103).

281. (S)   Report (Staff Summary Sheet), subject" "PAR Relay," 3 July 1971 by 7DOCPS in 7DOCPS files.

282. (S)   Davis Interview

283. (S)   Briefing/Conference, subject: "TFA Operations in COMMANDO HUNT VII," presented by Colonel Ben A. Barone, Director of Operations, TFA and Major Eric J. Brister, COMMANDO BOLT Operations Shop, TFA, to Colonel D. L. Flowers, Director of Command and Control, Hq 7AF, 18 September 1971

284. (S)   Ibid

285. (S)   Ibid

286. (S)   Interview, topic: Fusion Concept. With Colonel D. L. Evans, Director of Intelligence, TFA, by Captain Henry S. Shields, Project CHECO, 16 September 1971, at TFA, NKP RTAB, Thailand.

287. (S)   Report, subject: "Appendix IX to Annex EE (Anti-infiltration/IGLOO WHITE)," to COMMANDO HUNT VII Plan, 5 July 1971 by TFA. In 7DOCPS file.

288. (S)   Conversations with Colonel Ben A. Barone, Director of Operations, TFA by Captain Henry S. Shields, Project CHECO, 18 September 1971 at TFA, NKP RTAB, Thailand.

289. (S)   Study, subject: "Remote Ground Sensor Planning and Programming Objectives (REGSENSPO)," no date, by Hq USAF (CHECO Microfilm S442, FRs 142-143).

290. (S)   Letter Hq PACAF/XP to 7AF, 5AF, 13AF, 7/13AF, subject: "Ground Sensor Capabilities and Employment," 16 December 1970. Cover letter to Hq USAF REGSENSPO Document.

291. (S) Message 7XP to PACAF/XP, subject: "Ground Sensor Capabilities and Employment," 160702Z January 1971 (CHECO Microfilm S442, FRs 141-142). (Hereafter cited as 7AF Sensor Capabilities 160702Z January 1971 message).

292. (S) Ibid

293. (S) TFA History, 1 January-30 June 1970, p. 5

294. (S) 7AF Sensor Capabilities 160702Z January 1971 message.

295. (S) Ibid

296. (S) Letter, Hq PACAF/XPX to Hq USAF (XOXFT), subject: "Remote Ground Sensor Planning/Programming," 15 March 1971.

297. (S) Ibid

298. (U) John L. Frisbee, "IGLOO WHITE," Air Force Magazine, Vol 54, #6 (June 1971), pp. 48-53.

299. (C) Message, Det Eglin AFB, Florida to JCS/Sec Def Wash DC, subject: "CONUS Plan for Demonstration of a Ph IIIE System in Europe (MYSTIC MISSION)," 131230Z September 1971.

300. (S) Gathered from records on file in office of the Air Operations Division, Directorate of Operations, TFA, NKP RTAB, Thailand. Obtained 16 September 1971.

GLOSSARY

AAA	Antiaircraft Artillery
ABCCC	Airborne Battlefield Command and Control Center
ACOUSID	Acoustic Seismic Intrusion Detector
AC&W	Aircraft Control and Warning
ADSID	Air Delivered Seismic Intrusion Detector
AFSC	Air Force Systems Command
AMTI	Airborne Moving Target Indicator
ARDF	Airborne Radio Direction Finding
ARVN	Army of the Republic of Vietnam
ASR	Automatic Sequence Routing
ATA	Acoustic Targeting Area
BASS	Battlefield Area Surveillance System
BDA	Bomb Damage Assessment
CAEDET	Commandable Audio Engine Detector
CAP	Combat Air Patrol
CAS	Controlled American Source
COC	Combat Operations Center
COLOSSYS	Coordinated LORAN Sensor Strike System
COMMIKE	Commandable Microphone
COMUSMACV	Commander, United States Military Assistance Command, Vietnam
CONFIRM	Coincidence Filtering Intelligence Reporting Medium
CRC	Combat Reporting Center
DART	Deployable Automatic Relay Terminal
DASC	Direct Air Support Center
DCPG	Defense Communications Planning Group
DMPI	Desired Mean Point of Impact
DMZ	Demilitarized Zone
DO	Directorate of Operations (TFA)
DSPG	Defense Special Projects Group
ECM	Electronic Countermeasures
EDET	Engine Detector
ETA	Estimated Time of Arrival
FAC	Forward Air Controller
FADSID	Fighter Air-Delivered Seismic Intrusion Detector
FFV	Field Force Vietnam
GSM	Ground Surveillance Monitor

HANDSID	Hand-emplaced Seismic Intrusion Detector
HELOSID	Helicopters-emplaced Seismic Intrusion Detector
IN	Directorate of Intelligence (TFA)
ISC	Infiltration Surveillance Center
JGS	Joint General Staff
KIA	Killed in Action
LOC	Line of Communication
LORAN	Long Range Navigation
MACV	Military Assistance Command Vietnam
MAGID	Magnetic Intrusion Detector
MAW	Marine Air Wing
NOD	Night Observation Device
NULLO	No Live Operator Aboard
PAR	Palletized Airborne Relay
PIRID	Passive Intra-red Intrusion Detector
PMBR	Portable Multiple Bomb Rack
PMDL	Provisional Military Demarcation Line
PME	Prime Mission Equipment
RBA	Reconnaissance by Acoustic
REGSENSPO	Remote Ground Sensor Planning Objectives
RFI	Radio Frequency Interference
RTAFB	Royal Thai Air Force Base
RVN	Republic of Vietnam
RVNAF	Republic of Vietnam Armed Forces
RW	Reconnaissance Wing
SAM	Surface to Air Missile
SAR	Search and Rescue
SEA	Southeast Asia
SI	Special Intelligence
SOW	Special Operations Wing
SPIKEBUOY	Spike Acoubuoy
SPIKESID	Spike Seismic Intrusion Detector
SPOS	Strong Point Obstacle System
SRP	Sensor Reporting Post
SS	Security Squadron
SSS	Special Strike String
SSZ	Special Strike Zone
STOL	Short Take-off and Landing

TAC	Tactical Air Command
TACAIR	Tactical Air
TACP	Tactical Air Control Party
TAO	Traffic Assessment Officer
TFA	Task Force Alpha
TFS	Tactical Fighter Squadron
TIO	Targets Intelligence Officer
TO	Directorate of Engineering (TFA)
TOC	Tactical Operations Center
TOT	Time on Target
USAFE	United States Air Forces Europe
USAFSS	United States Air Force Security Service
VHF	Very High Frequency
VR	Visual Reconnaissance
WRZ	Western Reconnaissance Zone

RESEARCH NOTE

The period before 31 December 1970 covered in this report was largely based on the COMMANDO HUNT I, III, and V reports, the two previous CHECO IGLOO WHITE studies and material found in CHECO TOP SECRET Microfilm 98 and SECRET Microfilms 341, 346, 420, 435, 436, 437, and 442. Material for the period after 1 January 1971 was obtained from an examination of current files at TFA and the Surveillance Systems Branch, Tactical Air Control/Surveillance Division, Directorate of Command and Control, DCS/Operations (DOCPS) at Headquarters, Seventh Air Force, Tan Son Nhut Air Base, Republic of Vietnam. Interviews and conversations with TFA and DOCPS personnel were also used, as were the author's personal observations at TFA.